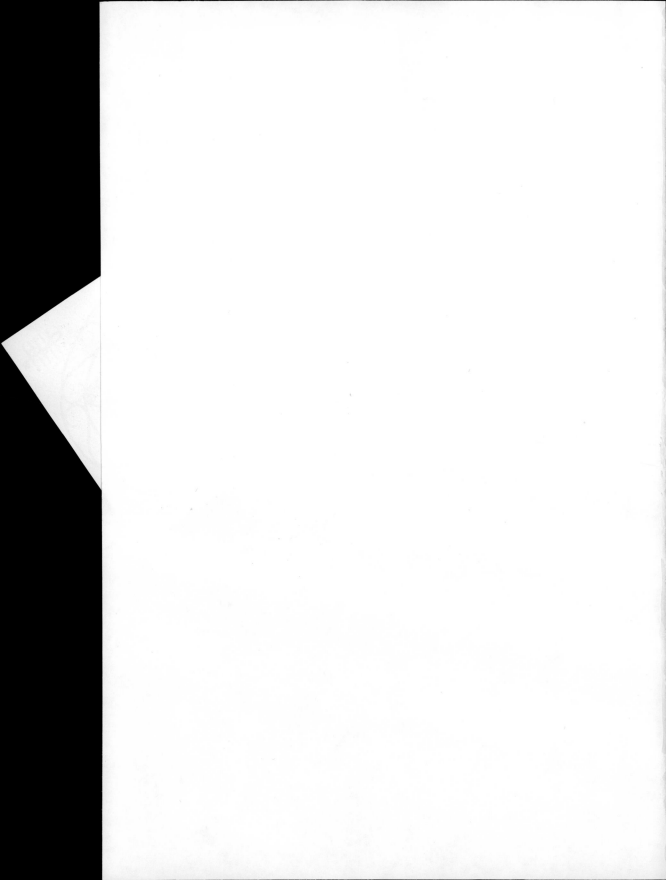

The Sword and The Pen

THE SWORD
AND THE PEN

Compiled and Edited by

MICHAEL BRANDER

LEO COOPER
London

First published 1989 by Leo Cooper

Leo Cooper is an independent imprint
of the Octopus Publishing Group Ltd,
Michelin House 81 Fulham Road, London SW3 6 RB

LONDON   MELBOURNE   AUCKLAND

A CIP catalogue record for this book
is available from the British Library

ISBN 0-85052-1106

Photoset by Rowland Phototypesetting Ltd
Bury St Edmunds, Suffolk
Printed in Great Britain by
St Edmundsbury Press Ltd, Bury St Edmunds, Suffolk
and bound by Hunter & Foulis Ltd, Edinburgh

Contents

Introduction

Twenty-one years ago I started the Leo Cooper imprint and this book is published to mark the anniversary. During that period some 500 titles have appeared under the logo of the sword and the pen, some good, some bad, but somehow the imprint has survived. However, on an occasion such as this, it is more appropriate to remember the successes than the failures. The winning of the W. H. Smith award in 1975 for Ronald Lewin's *Slim: The Standard Bearer* was one such shining star, as was the Governor General of Canada's award for Jeffery Williams's life of Lord Byng of Vimy. Two titles were awarded the Templar medal in successive years, one Lord Anglesey's fourth volume in his monumental five-volume work *A History of the British Cavalry*, the other Judge Babington's fine study of the courts-martial for cowardice in the First World War: *For the Sake of Example*. During these years we have also won the *Army Quarterly* Cup for Military History publishing and a number of other honours have been bestowed upon various hard-working authors.

I would like to thank Michael Brander for the work he has put into this selection, also Tim Jaques, the original designer of my colophon, and, above all, Tom Hartman, who has been responsible for editing virtually every book I have published. Mention too must be made of our trusted helpmate, Beryl Hill, who has served, on and off, for virtually the whole period that the imprint has survived.

Last, but not least, I would like to pay tribute to our authors, who have stuck by us through thick and thin – and there have indeed been some very thin times! Without them I would have had no books to publish and without their loyalty, support and advice I would not now be writing these words.

Leo Cooper

Acknowledgements

My thanks are due to many Librarians throughout the country who have assisted me with this book through the Inter-Library Lending System. In particular I must thank Miss Jessie Macleod, Librarian of the East Lothian District Library, also Mrs Veronica Wallace and others of the very helpful staff. My thanks must go to Mrs Gavan, the Librarian and always helpful staff of the Haddington Library. I must also thank very sincerely the Librarian and staff of the National Library of Scotland who are invariably courteous and helpful. Finally my thanks must go to the Librarian and staff of the War Museum Library who were also extremely helpful. All this may seem like straining at a gnat when only seven books, journals or manuscripts have been quoted at any length, but, of course, a great many more had to be read and checked before, for one reason or another, being discarded.

My thanks must go to Colonel D. R. B. Kaye, DSO, and his wife, for their painstaking research and copying of handwritten manuscripts, also for drawing my attention to Charles Godward's unpublished diary. I must also thank Mr J. D. Godward, his great-great-great-grandson, for permission to use extracts from his diary, and also Major D. J. H. Farquharson, Regimental Secretary of the 16th/5th The Queen's Royal Lancers, for his help in connection with regimental records. My thanks for permission to use their relatives' manuscripts must also go to the Coppard and Vaughan families.

My thanks are due to numerous people for reading and commenting on the text and for the tedious task of proof-reading, including, as ever, my wife Evelyn, also Mr K. H. Grose, Mr J. C. Clark and Mrs Laurie Maclennan, although for any mistakes or omissions I am entirely responsible.

My thanks must also go to Leo Cooper, a very understanding and co-operative publisher, something not always found in these days of the great conglomerates, who now celebrates the twenty-first anniversary of his own imprint and his well-known colophon, the crossed Sword and Pen.

Foreword

War in any shape or form arouses atavistic emotions in mankind. While the ambush is being planned, or the strategy of attack outlined, it still remains theoretical, but when the guns start firing it becomes a question of kill or be killed. For the junior officer or private soldier in the forefront of the battle war is a serious business, but he is the exception rather than the rule who records his experiences. Few men, when busy fighting, have either the time or the inclination, or even the means, to do so.

While there are many military reminiscences to choose from, almost all were written many years after the events portrayed. The diarists who cover service in action as a young man are very limited for obvious reasons. More often than not, if they kept a diary, neither it nor the diarist survived.

Although these widely contrasting records by both officers and private soldiers cover a time-span of over two centuries they have much in common. These were all perceptive young men at the sharp end of the action. Any one of them could have been killed at almost any time, with little real experience of life behind them. None of them were married, although a number had close ties with their families at home.

It is fascinating, therefore, to see how each faces up in much the same way to imminent action in which he may not only be killed but knows that his chances are poor. They have much in common also in their reactions when the shot and shell have ceased and the battlefield is silent. On other aspects, such as their attitudes to looting and plunder, to the troops opposing them, to being wounded or sick, to the generals who are leading them, to the people on whom they are billeted and many other points they often hold strangely similar views across the centuries, despite the differences in warfare and in the military background.

It can be seen that war poses problems for the individual unlikely to be encountered in any other circumstances. In a sense it liberates him from ordinary rules and conventions, but forces him to make his own life or death decisions affecting himself, his companions, or the enemy. Fear comes in many forms and he learns to control or conceal it. In the stress of war there are formative, sometimes soul-searing, experiences and it is interesting to see each man developing visibly in his diary.

Modern technology might appear to have altered war and a soldier's life beyond recognition over the past two centuries or so, but in some ways the lot of a soldier in action has not changed so very greatly. Many of his attitudes are likely to be similar to those portrayed, while his experiences mark him indelibly for life, whether he realizes it at the time or not. So it was with the young men whose records are quoted.

One of the interesting features of these records is how much they often have in common with the experiences of others in different wars and different parts of the world and even in different centuries. The veteran of Vietnam or Korea will recognize similarities between his war and that of the East India Company officer, whose journal so vividly portrays war in Asia at the turn of the 18th century, and with the other two mid-19th century soldiers in India. The veteran of the desert war, or the war in Europe, will recall similarities between his experiences, while advancing or retreating, and those of the Peninsular campaign veterans whose diaries are quoted. Anyone will recognize the horrors of war portrayed in the last two diaries.

These diaries span over two centuries of warfare and it is really only in weapons technology that there is any great change to be found today. The differences between being killed by a solid cannon ball or new-fangled rifle or shrapnel shell in the Peninsular campaign are little different from death by a Kalashnikov or a rocket. The end result is a mangled bloody corpse either way. Tanks and jet planes, nerve gases and nuclear bombs may now have made full-scale war almost unthinkable, but Israeli soldiers, Syrian troops, Lebanese militia men and Kurdish villagers, to name only a few of those currently engaged in armed struggles, are still fighting hand to hand in the last resort. They too would recognize the reactions and emotions portrayed in these diaries.

In the end, if a war has to be fought, it is the young men who are inevitably involved. Their attitudes and emotions will at times be similar to those so well portrayed by those young men whose diaries and journals are quoted. Also well portrayed are the effects of war and its perpetual out-riders – pestilence, poverty and lawlessness – on the civilian population.

War sees a timeless slaughter of the innocent, when innocence itself is lost. If nothing else, in these pages the pen is proved a great deal sharper than the sword.

CHAPTER ONE

Lieutenant John Pester
1778–1856
Journal in India: 1802–1806

'If an officer would wish to *get forward* he should pray for opportunities
to distinguish himself and let none escape him that offer.'

John Pester was born in 1778, the younger son of a Somerset squire. It is
clear from his diaries that from an early age he was a keen shot and rider to
hounds, never afraid of taking his own line across country. With the
example of Clive fresh in the public mind, India no doubt seemed the land
of opportunity to the sons of proud if impecunious squires. Through

I

family connections and influence he obtained a commission in a native regiment in India, clearly attracted by the sports of the country, such as pig-sticking and big game hunting, which he enjoyed to the full. At the same time, as his diary makes plain, he was a professional soldier of the Georgian period, full of reckless courage and determined to gain promotion in the field or die in the attempt.

From 1802 until 1806, aged between 24 and 28, he kept a journal of his experiences when serving with the army in India. His diary is among the earliest of those kept by officers serving in India and gives a unique insight into the effects of a tropical climate and disease on even the hardiest of constitutions. The Georgian attitudes to warfare were refreshingly simple and life was lived to the full. 'Bottom', or personal courage, was rated extremely highly and on this count alone it is clear that John Pester was greatly admired by his fellow officers as well as by his men.

His diaries start without preamble when he was already a Lieutenant in the 1st Battalion of the Bengal Native Infantry, soon to be involved in the Second Mahratta War, the campaign during which General Arthur Wellesley was to demonstrate his formidable qualities as a tactician for the first time. Pester's opening paragraph is typical of the man. He began:

'August 28th: In consequence of the refractory conduct of some Zemindars who had been committing sad depredations and setting the laws of government at defiance I was ordered to march with my Grenadiers this evening. My friend Marsden expressed a wish to accompany me and waited on Colonel Blair who readily consented.'

John Pester paraded his men 'at four in the afternoon' to check 'their arms, flints, ammunition, bayonets, etc', then he led them off at five through 'thirty-two long miles' of flooded country up to the soldiers' waists. At four in the morning they arrived at the village of Assnayder, two miles from the rebels' strongly-held position in the fortified village of Camney. He galloped forward with his guides and reconnoitred the ground. Then, setting Marsden in command of a party attacking one gate, he led his own party to assault the other:

'The enemy's fire was not returned until we reached the sorties, when I ordered the rear division of my party to fire on the enemy whilst with the other division I forced the gates, which with the greatest difficulty we happily effected. The instant we entered the village my men were like so many tigers let loose. . . . I discovered a round tower pierced with loopholes . . . here a party of the more resolute had retired. . . . This was no season for delay. . . . I collected about thirty men, and, with my Subadar (black captain) I rushed on at their head to assault the post . . . four of my grenadiers were shot at my heels. . . . We succeeded in getting so close under them they could not fire upon us. . . . Marsden . . . joined me here . . . the enemy heard that we proposed digging them out and instantly . . . surrendered. . . . We now fired the village in every quarter and many of the enemy who had secreted themselves were destroyed. By our best calculation nearly two hundred of them fell in this affair and we had reason to conjecture that in future they would treat us with more respect.'

He then turned back towards the village of Assnayder which had been his base for the attack, but, hearing that there was a threat to rescue his prisoners, he took up a strategic position and ordered 'the Sergeant of the Guard who had charge of the prisoners to put them immediately to death if we should be attacked'. They stood to arms ready for an attack for a full hour and, rather apologetically, he then noted: 'My men were much exhausted; it was now nearly eleven in the morning and we had been positively marching and engaged full sixteen hours.'

When they finally reached Assnayder again, he and Marsden and their troops were provided with food by the villagers: 'more, I fancy, from dread of us than any good wishes towards us'.

He recorded: 'To Marsden and myself they brought eggs, milk, and a very fine kid which we had for breakfast, and about three we took a kid chop and a bottle of claret each (which Major Collins had very kindly sent after us). This we enjoyed much, though Marsden fell asleep the moment we had swallowed our wine.'

At five in the evening he started back for Shikoabad, where they were based, and encountered a fearsome thunderstorm which forced them to take shelter in an old fort until five in the morning. He wrote:

'At seven we arrived in cantonments, beating the Grenadiers' march. All the men in wonderful spirits considering the extreme fatigue they had borne. . . . I dismissed my men on their own parade and waited immediately on Colonel Blair, who . . . told me that we had done our duty in a manner very much to our credit. . . . Marsden and myself breakfasted with the Colonel and afterwards retired to our own bungalows to get a little rest of which we stood in much need. (Poor Marsden never recovered this fatigue, and died soon afterwards.)'

It is indicative of John Pester's constitution that he does not appear to have been greatly affected, although he noted: 'In the evening I dined at Plumer's, when there was a large party, and as soon as the cloth was removed I fell asleep in my chair and slept undisturbed till nearly eleven o'clock, after which I took my bottle of claret and retired to my palanquin.'

By November the revolt had spread and on 2 November he recorded: 'Prepared everything this evening for marching, and as we were in expectation of a tedious campaign I carried with me a good stock of wines.'

He went on: 'November 25th. The Battalion paraded this morning at daybreak. . . . The country today which we marched over I was thoroughly acquainted with having very often beat every inch of it for game.'

By 30 November they were camping near the town of Etah. There he saw a large lake and 'after a hasty breakfast' he and his friend Cumberledge:

'Took our guns and had a famous morning's sport. . . . By four in the evening we had killed twenty-three brace of snipe and this was one of the prettiest day's sport I had seen in India. . . . On our return we killed four brace of teal and three ducks. . . . This being the anniversary of Saint Andrew, a day always kept by Scotchmen, we dined at MacKaulay's to whom we had sent all the game. . . . We mustered very strong . . . as nearly all the Scotch in the camp were invited. . . . We paid them the compliment of pushing the bottle handsomely and the whole party was pretty high when we separated.'

Their immediate objective was to take the town of Sarssney, the seat of one of the rebel Rajahs, but the approach march was unhurried and during one halt of a few days he noted that Cumberledge and he were able to go out shooting on several occasions and 'found hares, peafowl, quail, black and grey partridges in great abundance and never returned without filling our bags!'

Finally they approached the heavily fortified town of Sarssney. After negotiations with the Rajah had failed to produced any result, on 23 December they began the siege in the approved manner with working parties digging trenches and siege artillery being brought into action. Their first move was to capture two villages in front of Sarssney:

'My Company (and a party of pioneers under Lieutenant Bates with us to assist us) were pushed on to a grove in front. We instantly formed working parties . . . and at daybreak our trenches were completed after as hard a night's fagging as I ever knew.'

John Pester was soon involved in action, as he recorded in his usual racy style:

'We remained snug in our works till about the middle of the day. . . . About two o'clock a tremendous fire of cannon suddenly opened on our trench, and at the same moment about five hundred of the enemy rushed out sword in hand from a very high field of corn upon our flank. I . . . instantly ordered my own Company not to fire a shot without orders from me, at the same time I stepped out of the trench and went to the officer commanding the other Company. . . . I did not find this officer in a situation much to his credit. The cannon shot, which came in showers about the trench . . . seemed to have scared him . . . he exclaimed that "if I did not come into the trench I should be killed," taking special care . . . to keep very close to the bottom of it. . . . I then gave *his men* the orders I had my own, and returned to my post. Our soldiers received them with the greatest coolness and gallantry and we repulsed them with great slaughter. . . .

'My Company of Grenadiers . . . behaved as well as men could do . . . and Major Ball, the field officer of the day . . . assured us that he would report the "meritorious conduct" of the two Companies . . . to the Commanding Officer.'

The siege then continued with the artillery brought into action until a breach could be made in the defences. By 14 January the breach had been duly made and it was decided that a storming party should be mounted. On 15 January, along with a Lieutenant Sinclair, John Pester was deputed to lead the storming of this breach. 'The stormers to consist of all the Grenadier companies of the detachment; my company . . . to lead.' His friend Wemyss, whose brother was General Wemyss, 'came down the moment the orders were issued to take a glass of wine with us and shake me by the hand.' John Pester's description of the storming of the breach is riveting. There was a false attack on the north gate to draw the defenders' attention away, while Pester's force advanced in bright moonlight. He wrote vividly:

'We had nearly reached the glacis before the enemy discovered us. . . . A galling fire now commenced upon us. Forty soldiers with the scaling ladders . . . preceded my section, which led the column. . . . Everything depended on our placing the scaling ladders with precision. . . . The first ladder I placed myself – our men were now dropping on every side of us. Sinclair and myself descended the two first ladders which we placed in the ditch, and instantly turned them and mounted on the fort side . . . but how shall I describe my feelings when I found the ladders would not reach the top by nearly *ten feet!* . . . A little to my right I observed the wall was somewhat shattered. . . . I got across from the top of one ladder to another, and with every exertion, unencumbered as I was, I reached the top of the wall alone. . . . My sword was slung by the sword-knot round my wrist and I had both hands to scramble for it. My favourite havildar . . . was endeavouring to ascend with me when he was shot, and his blood flew completely over me. . . . I pistolled the man who was nearest to me, and who was in the act of cutting at me with his sabre; several muskets were fired at me by men actually not fifteen paces from me! but I had scarcely got my footing on the wall when a musket shot grazed my arm just above the wrist, a spear at the same time wounded me in the shoulder and a grenade (which they were showering upon us) struck me a severe blow on the breast, and hurled me almost breathless backwards from the wall. The men in the ladders caught me, but on seeing me fall exclaimed that I was shot. I soon recovered my breath. The fire upon us was extremely heavy . . . and our men dropped fast out of the ladders.'

The storming party remained in 'this mortifying predicament' for a quarter of an hour before being ordered to retreat. He and Sinclair were at the top of the storming ladders and were the last to leave. They had thirty feet to descend and the same height to ascend again on the other side, 'all of which time they were firing and spearing at us from a distance not exceeding fifteen yards!' He described the scene in these terms:

'Many of the soldiers mounting the ladders to clear the ditch over our heads were shot and came falling down upon us and numberless shot and spears came on every side . . . we had to walk over the killed and wounded with which the bottom was strewed . . . but . . . reached the sand side of the ditch. . . . As I returned from the fort towards our trenches there appeared . . . literally a shower of ball, and the men retreating in my front were falling very thick . . . from weakness and loss of blood I returned but very slowly.'

In the end he reached the safety of the trenches where he found his brother officer Sinclair already returned. Then came the aftermath, the congratulations on a miraculous escape and the parade of the remainder of the company:

'Major Ball came instantly to us and . . . congratulated us upon our very extraordinary escape. . . . Sinclair had no less than ten shot holes in his hat! The wound in my shoulder was by no means deep as the weapon ran up under the skin and came out upon the top of the shoulder; a musket shot passed through the cuff of my jacket and took a little of the skin of my arm with it. As soon as I was able to collect the men I paraded my Company and it made my heart ache to find that of eighty gallant fellows who marched down to the attack with me forty-three had fallen!'

Then followed the inevitable enquiries and recriminations on this fiasco. According to the engineer officers the ditch had been sounded but allowance had not been made for the depth of mud, nor for the fact that the wall of the fort stood six feet or more above that of the glacis. However, Sinclair and John Pester were praised by the Commanding Officer 'in a manner most gratifying to our feelings', and word of the affair also went back to the Commander-in-Chief at headquarters.

This was by no means the only time he distinguished himself in action during this siege. On 20 January he was stationed in the rear when the enemy made a sortie on the trenches from the fort via the jungle on the flank. The same captain who had cowered in the trench next to him was sent to repel them and then John Pester was sent to support him with sixty men. He recorded:

'About half-way between the jungle and our post I observed the captain . . . retreating *very precipitately*. . . . he assured me very earnestly that it was impossible to remain out, the fire from the guns of the fort was so heavy. I made him no reply but pushed on to the jungle and took post at the spot he had quitted, where we . . . fortunately succeeded in driving the enemy out . . . under very heavy fire from twelve pieces of cannon from the garrison. I then formed my men again upon the skirt of the jungle, when the enemy began to press on me in great numbers. . . . All this had been observed in the lines and Major Ball came down with all possible expedition with a gun and three hundred men to support me. On observing this . . . we instantly charged to the front and the enemy ran . . . in all directions before us.'

The artillery sergeant who was aiming the gun was then killed, but John Pester had studied gunnery and was able to lay the gun successfully, so that the enemy were repulsed with considerable losses. He ended his account with the note: 'We were relieved this evening by the 2nd Battalion of our regiment. I had a late dinner at Cunyinghame's, where we spent a very jolly evening and did real justice to his claret.'

It is scarcely surprising, in view of his obvious gallantry in action, that

Pester's own views on his profession matched his conduct in the field. He wrote forthrightly:

'I am convinced that if an officer would wish to *get forward* he should pray for opportunities to distinguish himself and let none escape him that offer. To be first and foremost in danger should be his object; if he falls, he falls gallantly and respected and it is a thousand to one if he is not rewarded should he succeed in doing his duty in the *style of a soldier.*'

It is understandable that, living up to such ideals, as he obviously did, must have made him an uncomfortable – even if widely admired – acquaintance for the less committed amongst his fellows. On the other hand it is satisfying to know that he did in fact get his just rewards for his conduct at the siege of Sarssney.

On 28 January, recording the visit of HE the Commander-in-Chief, General Lake, he noted:

'I met the Commander-in-Chief this evening at dinner and his Excellency asked me a great number of questions . . . and told me that my conduct . . . had been "reported to him in a manner much to my credit," . . . I was much flattered by the attention which the General . . . showed me. His Excellency during dinner remarked . . . "I will take care that the ladders shall be long enough the next time you are in the breach."'

The following day he was detailed to accompany General Lake while reconnoitring the fort. The General appears to have been every bit as reckless of danger as John Pester, who recorded:

'His Excellency in order to have as near a view of the works as possible was at the head of our column and not twenty paces in my front when a cannon shot grazed close at his horse's fore feet; the animal . . . reared and fell back with the General, but . . . he received no other accident but a sprained foot and being otherwise a good deal bruised. Within three minutes afterwards another shot came and took my horse just behind the ribs and close to the centre of the saddle, cutting his *completely in two.* This was a happy escape for me!

'We at last drew off from the garrison, but lost many men before we got without reach of the guns. This was the first specimen we had of General Lake's intrepidity.'

The siege of the fort ended quite tamely with the garrison withdrawing under cover of darkness, more or less by tacit agreement, since the military objective was to take the fort rather than to kill the enemy. Thus on 7 February the British force occupied the fort and the first thing John Pester and several of his friends did was check the length of the ladders used in his attack which they found had been drawn up and stored in the fort. They were found to be eight feet too short and Pester not unnaturally decided on 'reporting the particulars . . . to Major Ball who commanded the storming party'.

They spent only a week in occupation of Sarssney and Pester noted: 'It was with some regret that we left Sarssney and our princely quarters. . . . Livesey and myself had taken possession of the . . . Zenanah part . . . allotted for the ladies, but to our regret they had all been carried off.'

The night before their departure they decided to throw a dinner party in the Zenanah and Livesey and Pester invited a dozen guests, including Colonel Blair, their Commanding Officer. Pester recorded:

'It was the last night we were to pass in Sarssney and I believe the first that ever fourteen *honest gentlemen* drank within its walls. Three dozen and a half of claret, and proportionable quantity of Madeira – everyone sang his song and this was as gay an evening and terminated as pleasantly as any I passed in my life. We concluded by breaking our candle-shades and glasses, pranks which too frequently finish drinking parties in this quarter of the globe.'

They did not have far to march to their next encampment outside another fort that had recently fallen. Here Livesey and he inspected the fort, then indulged in some hare-coursing: 'We found a hare close to our piquet and killed her in front of the line after an uncommon severe run.' Not content with this, Pester noted; 'In the evening Peyron of the 3rd Cavalry . . . and myself took our guns and walked about two miles. . . . We shot a very large buck antelope, several brace of quail and partridge and three hares.'

It was by no means all play, however, for the next day he and his friend Livesey were in action with their companies under severe fire from enemy cannon. The following day John Pester was able to demonstrate his skill in firing a cannon again and effectively silenced two of the enemy guns. On 21 February he led his company into action again, successfully storming the breach of a fortress they were attacking, although wounded in the leg in the process. He described it thus:

'At the foot of the breach I received a graze in my leg, but managed to ascend to the top of it, when I sent Campbell and the Europeans to take possession of the gates. . . . With my small party we kept possession of the breach and the gateways. After everything was over and the firing had completely ceased . . . I gave Campbell his orders and in a dooley [stretcher] returned to the camp, as I found my wound was very painful, though, as I was able to stand I was quite sure the bone of the leg could not be injured. The surgeon assured me that with care and proper diet in one month I would be quite recovered.'

This proved to be the last action of this campaign and the army remained halted until 19 March, by which time John Pester was indeed almost completely recovered. The army was then dispersed and Pester was given two months leave. He decided to make up a hunting party with various friends in the 3rd Cavalry, in particular his close friend Peyron, also from Somerset. They were fortunate to be given good sporting facilities by a civilian friend named Thornhill who lived at Bareilly and provided them with elephants for tiger-shooting.

They clearly had considerable sport shooting tigers from the howdahs of elephants with guns loaded with 'double-headed' shot, and Pester was moved to comment: 'There is something to a person not in the habit of killing tigers, so awful . . . in their charge, that it is apt to shake the hand a little. . . . I cannot otherwise account for a tiger ever being missed at a near distance.'

By this time he was completely recovered and distinguished himself at pig-sticking. He noted: 'With a hard-mouthed ungovernable horse hog-hunting is by far the most dangerous sport of any I ever engaged in and there are few instances of a large boar and a horse coming in contact without either the horse or his rider being much cut and frequently the horse is killed on the spot. Our ground today was very dangerous, full of holes and old wells and many of them quite covered with grass which grew over them. In these cases it is usual to follow the exact trail of the hog. . . . An experienced hunter always sticks as close after them as possible and by so doing very often saves his bones. Hog hunting beyond a doubt requires the most desperate riding.'

After two months of tiger-shooting, hog-hunting and shooting every kind of game as well as wining and dining with his numerous friends, Pester's leave finally ended and he returned by 1 June to his regiment at Shikoabad. He then appears to have had an attack of malaria just as his Company was ordered into action. He recorded:

'The Colonel wrote me a most kindly note, strongly advising me, in my present state, not to think of marching with the Detachment. . . . I thanked him in the kindest terms I could, but told him that, as my Company was under orders, I should assuredly march with it. (Memo: – Never to remain behind on these occasions.)'

Despite his determination not to miss the chance of action it is clear that John Pester was extremely ill. He wrote: 'The fever continued severely on me during the night and I believe that I drank at least a gallon of water.' In spite of this he appears to have figured prominently in the action the next day, leading his men in the capture of a village and an attack on a fort. He wrote, however: 'I never suffered greater pain than I did this afternoon; the exertion in the early part of the day had increased my headache and fever exceedingly,' After the fort was taken he noted laconically: 'No plunder was found . . . of any consequence. The fever continued to distress me during the day.'

This was apparently his first bout of malaria and thereafter he was to suffer regularly from its debilitating effects, his health gradually deteriorating. However, his life at the battalion base at Shikoabad continued with rounds of parties interspersed with sporting outings and troop exercises.

The preponderance of Scots amongst his fellow officers is shown by this entry:

'Sinclair, Grant, Livesey, Weston, Macgregor, Forbes, Murray, Arden, Harriott, Vaughan and Macaulay dined with me this evening and we kept it up till an *early hour*. Sung a great deal and parted in high good humour. Some of the party who absconded after drinking as long as they thought proper were brought back to the charge, and this ended in one of the *hardest going* days I ever saw in my life.'

He noted next morning: 'We paraded (some of us, others reported sick) at gun-fire this morning for exercise.' The following day news reached them of an uprising of native troops and also of an attack by the Scindian Brigades in the Deccan. On 15 August he recorded: 'Got up this morning an hour before daybreak and saw my tent and baggage all laden on the camels and bullocks. At gunfire we paraded . . . at six we marched out of cantonments in the highest spirits possible. We encamped not more than two miles from our cantonment.'

On 19 August he recorded interestingly: 'The half-caste officers of Scindiah's service had left it in consequence of a proclamation declaring that all people of that description, born of British parentage who remained in the service of native powers, with whom war was now declared, would be considered as traitors to their country and treated accordingly should the fate of war throw them into our hands.'

When the army assembled General Lake, the Commander-in-Chief, sent for Pester's commanding officer and informed him he wished to promote Pester to be Brigade Quartermaster on the staff. The Scindian forces were commanded by General Perron, a Frenchman, and Pester noted: 'The French officers, of course, remained attached to General Perron, but after the proclamation which had been issued it would have been treason in Englishmen to have continued and to have fought against their own country.' (In effect this was really an extension of the war in Europe with the French leading native troops against British-led native troops.)

Despite his new staff appointment John Pester still managed to get in the forefront of the first battle on 20 August, when the French-led army was routed decisively. On 2 September he noted: 'In the night we experienced the severe shock of an earthquake . . . the motion was very like that of a small boat in a moderate sea.'

On 3 September he mentioned receiving letters which reported hostilities having started in the Deccan and that 'General Wellesley had taken . . . the fort of Ahmidnagur by storm.' The following day, by General Lake's orders, he accompanied the storming party in the attack on General Perron's fort. He was in the thick of it as ever and wrote: 'My horse was twice wounded this morning, but I, with my usual good fortune, escaped unhurt.' As soon as the storming party was successful he reported the news to the General and returned with him to the fort, where there were numerous casualties, including some close friends. He noted casually: 'The storming party were allowed three hours to plunder and we found several tumbrils of treasure in the garrison.'

There followed a gloomy evening when many of his friends were buried with military ceremony. It was learned that while the regiment had been engaged in capturing the enemy fort another force had attacked their base at Shikoabad. Although repulsed with heavy losses, it had burned all the bungalows with their possessions and furniture. However, he was somewhat cheered up by General Lake informing him that he would shortly be given a better appointment than Quartermaster.

On 11 September John Pester wrote:

'Soon after daybreak I observed two men . . . endeavouring to avoid us. I pursued them with a couple of troopers and soon came up with them.

The men . . . confessed they were from the enemy's camp . . . they had been led to suppose that we were not arrived at Secundia. . . . They told us that Scindiah's army composed of fourteen thousand men and one hundred pieces of cannon was . . . within *five miles* drawn up in order of battle. . . . The Quarter Master General did not credit this account. . . . The men were put under guard, an account of their report was sent back . . . and we proceeded . . . marking out the ground of encampment. . . . At this period we did not know that the enemy's line was within *a mile and a half* of us, nor had they the smallest idea of us being within fifteen miles of them.'

This sort of scenario is one that is familiar to any soldier who has ever been in action. The British army was pitching tents and the men were undressed and dismissed when the advanced piquets encountered the enemy and the drums started to beat to arms. Pester as usual was in the vanguard of the action. He had one horse killed under him but he quickly mounted a replacement and when they had advanced within 250 yards of the enemy's guns he remained the only mounted officer in front of the ranks. He wrote;

'I saw the left a little staggered and was pushing down to encourage them when General Saint John from the rear, who did not observe me, gave the word to "Fire" and, most miraculous to say, I escaped unhurt although I was actually within *twelve yards* of the front rank men, at full speed, when the whole gave their fire. The volley was instantly followed by a cheer and . . . they rushed on with an ardour nothing could resist . . . the enemy had greatly the advantage of us in running.'

The enemy were soon in full flight. General Lake came round to congratulate his men but it was sunset before they finally started setting out their encampment. Pester wrote:

'A drink of muddy water given me by a drummer of the 2nd Battalion . . . almost saved my life after the close of the action. . . . We had been twelve hours in as scorching a sun as ever shone from the heavens and nearly *eighteen hours* marching and in action.'

He was ordered to post a guard on the General Hospital tents and recorded: 'About thirty surgeons were absolutely covered with blood. . . . In one corner of the tent stood a pile of legs and arms, from which the boots and clothes of many were not yet stripped off.'

During this action on the banks of the River Jumnah, Pester calculated that the British had only seven thousand men and eight guns against seventeen thousand men and a hundred guns. Yet the enemy were driven back across the Jumnah at the point of the bayonet. They even failed to destroy the bridge of boats they had made across the river.

A few days after the victory John Pester played 'Hazard' in the lines of the 12th battalion: 'We played till sunset and played deep. We were fortunate and returned across the Jumnah £150 more worth than in the morning.'

Inside a week they were on the march again and Pester described one of the irritations of Indian warfare: 'Several alarms were given during the march that banditti were plundering the baggage . . . about thirty of the vagabonds were shot. . . . Grant of ours lost his trunks containing his clothes and his wine this morning (no small annoyance to an officer marching in an enemy's country where neither one nor the other can be procured.)'

Throughout this period it is clear that the General had his eye on him for possible promotion, but John Pester was kept busy with the Quarter-master General's staff during the advance on Agra. There he again had several narrow escapes. When the garrison capitulated, Pester recorded: 'I had the inexpressible satisfaction with my own hands to haul down the Scindiah's colours and plant the British Standard in its stead.' He added: 'The treasure found in the garrison . . . amounted to twenty four lacks [*sic*: a lakh equals a hundred thousand rupees] and forty-four thousand rupees. NB – I expect six thousand (equal to £800) to be my share.'

Although he applied for further active service, much to his disgust Pester was forced to remain behind with his regiment as aide to his Colonel. General Lake, however, had not forgotten him and finally relented, promoting him to Brigade Major of the 4th Brigade at the end of October. On 1 November they attacked the enemy force successfully and defeated them, although with considerable casualties.

There followed a peaceful interlude, when hog-hunting and sport predominated. By January, however, they were preparing to besiege Gwalior, a fortress deemed almost impregnable, standing on a very steep-sided rock. Inevitably John Pester was in the forefront of the action, having numerous narrow escapes while reconnoitring the ground. Pester greatly admired the courage of his Commanding Officer, Brigadier White, but on this occasion the odds seemed so hopeless that even he seemed on the point of giving up. However, Pester persuaded him at least to make a do-or-die attack and they were about to storm the breach, with

Pester to the fore, when the enemy surrendered. Even Pester was prepared to admit that the attack would have been a desperate affair, but Brigadier White did not fail to mention him in glowing terms in a subsequent despatch to General Lake.

For the whole of February Pester was involved in administrative duties in Gwalior, a notably unhealthy spot; then in March he became dangerously ill with a fever and nearly died. His diary ceased completely until the end of April when he was strong enough to sit up for a quarter of an hour at a time. The doctors suggested he should go on sick leave, but still being on active service he refused to take their advice, although the temperature was over 125 degrees and one evening the candles on the dinner table melted! He noted in a moment of uncharacteristic gloom 'men dropping off daily'.

Towards the end of May Brigadier White thought he might be ordered into action. Pester wrote: 'The Brigadier asked me if in my present weakly state I would accompany him, to which I most readily assented, though the medical men *comforted* me by telling me that to attempt to take the field in my reduced state in such a season would inevitably prove fatal.'

By 1 June, however, even Pester had realized that a period of recuperation was necessary and he agreed to take sick leave. On 2 June he recorded: 'arrived at Gohud about six, where I found my tent ready pitched in a fine mango grove and breakfast on the table. I found great relief from the burning rock of Gwalior to a fine, fertile country, and the trees completely shading my tent made it tolerably cool.'

On 3 June at his next, less pleasantly placed camp, he recorded: 'I . . . daily gained a little strength . . . at four I dined, drank my pint of claret and sent on my tent and luggage.' On 5 June he was evidently improving and noted enthusiastically: 'at daylight reached, and *once again crossed the Jumnah* . . . made a very hearty breakfast.'

By 14 July he was approaching Bareilly and much recovered, when he encountered his old friends Peyron and Anderdon tiger hunting. He promptly joined them and personally accounted for the man-eater they were hunting with a shot through the eye. He was obviously getting better, although far from recovering his full health.

On 26 July he made this entry: 'A report that the army will take the field immediately. The surgeons advised me not to think of marching in my present weak state of health, but I resolved, the consequence be what it may, to leave Bareilly the moment General Lake marches from

Cawnpore.' Nevertheless on 30 July he recorded: 'Coursed this morning, but a smart gallop after the first hare we found gave me so severe a headache that I was obliged to leave the party and return home.'

On 31 July he had a recurrence of fever and was unable to write in his diary until 7 August, but by 14 August he was coursing at daybreak and 'had five of the best runs I ever saw . . . returned as much fatigued as I ever had been.' Two days later, however, he was shooting deer, hogs and partridges and by 23 August he was obviously much recovered and on 25 August he received a letter from his friend Wemyss warning him 'to prepare immediately to take the field'. He noted: 'I resolved on joining the army, and not to go back to a sickly garrison as Gwalior was well known to be, many fatal proofs of which I had witnessed. The general orders left it optional to me, as absent by leave on a sick certificate, either to remain at Bareilly, return to my Brigade Majorship at Gwalior, or join. I determined, of course, on the latter, though very much against the advice of the medical men . . . they assured me seriously that by marching at this season I . . . endangered my life. But I had not been accustomed to remain behind on such occasions and therefore told them my resolve to risk everything and to join the army.'

On 4 September he left Bareilly and joined his friends the Cunynghames at Mynpoorie, noting laconically: 'We passed a very pleasant day and I was less annoyed by the headache than I had for many days been.' On 10 September he reached Agra and there waited for General Lake's arrival from Cawnpore, noting: 'As I was daily annoyed with pain of my side and head and every symptom of the liver complaint I was advised to return again into garrison, as it was much cooler in a house than in a tent and not to expose myself until it was indispensably necessary.'

On 18 September his old friend Wemyss on General Lake's staff wrote to him with the welcome news that he was promised a Brigade Majorship and that his old appointment at Gwalior remained, so that after the campaign he might return to it, which was just as he had wished.

On 20 September he was asked to give his advice on reconnoitring an enemy advance and came under fire again in a short but sharp action. On 24 September General Lake arrived and before the question of the Brigade Majorship was settled Pester was persuaded by his friends to 'come forward as a candidate for the prize agency . . . and as it would be most gratifying to be chosen for that honourable station by the officers of the army, I determined to try it.' [The post of Prize Agent was chosen by popular vote and was regarded as a signal honour.]

On 26 September he wrote: 'I never experienced an anxiety to what I felt on this occasion, for I considered that to be chosen by a majority of officers of the army was an honour that any man might be proud of and would be a most convincing proof that one's conduct had gained their notice and approbation. I had the satisfaction of seeing many an officer's name down for me to whom I had considered I was a perfect stranger.' The following day he was down in brigade orders as Prize Agent for Native Infantry.

On 1 October at the camp, he 'suffered extremely by the headache.' He was clearly still far from recovered. On 8 October he noted: 'I found myself extremely feverish and hardly able to sit on my horse.' This did not stop him having a sharp brush with a large party of the enemy forces who were intent on attacking an ammunition convoy. He routed them smartly in full view of General Lake. He then stood to arms all night, but had no further action, being relieved at dawn on the 5th. Not surprisingly he recorded: 'October 6th. The morning was as usual dreadfully hot and I was very unwell; did not quit my tent all day.'

On 7 October he was in action again, and again on 10 October. Then on the 12th, after a difficult day's march in the face of the enemy, he went down with a raging fever from which he was expected to die, but, with his remarkable constitution, he pulled through and began to keep his diary again on the 25th, by which time he was ensconced in Delhi with the army, having been taken there semi-delirious. On the 26th he noted: 'Continued swallowing bark (quinine) in great quantities and still remain exceedingly weak.'

By 5 November he was well enough to march with the army and by the 12th they soundly defeated the enemy, although with considerable loss. No further action took place until December when, on the night of the 7th, Pester was engaged guarding a party of pioneers whose task was to break the dam of a large lake with a view to flooding a fortress they were attacking. In the morning he was satisfied to see 'a great deal of the ground on the east face of the fort under water and the enemy endeavouring in vain to stop it'.

On the 10th, in charge of the flankers during a jungle march, he had numerous narrow escapes and 'found myself much annoyed by a violent headache in consequence of having exerted myself . . . in the morning.'

This did not stop him on the next day leading three Companies in a highly successful surprise attack on a large body of the enemy.

The usual preparations for a siege followed and on 20 December he recorded: 'I had as narrow escape this afternoon as ever I had in my life . . . a cannon shell grazed on the top of the trench, took the bearskin of my hat, tore it to pieces and lodged in the parapet . . . it was within half a foot of carrying away both Durant's legs. . . . This escape was a very providential one to us both and . . . *mutual congratulations* followed.'

By the 23rd the breach was ready for storming and the attack duly took place successfully, but many of Pester's friends in his battalion were killed or severely wounded, among the latter his Somerset friend Anderdon. Only six officers including himself were now left from the original eighteen. This did not stop Pester from leading a successful charge the following day when his friend Colonel Ball was severely wounded while planning the attack.

'I was with Brigadier MacRie and Colonel Haldane at the head of the column; several men were shot around us, but we all escaped. I advanced with MacRie for, as prize agent, I considered it a point of duty to be foremost in order to secure any property that may fall into our hands and to prevent the soldiers plundering it.' The next day, (Christmas Day, although no mention of the fact is made in his diaries) Pester was ready to take part in storming the fortress, but it was discovered that the enemy had withdrawn in the night.

'The gates we found jarring open. . . . I posted my Grenadiers on the ramparts and with my own hands planted our Battalion colours on the . . . principal flagstaff on which we found the Rajah's standard still flying. . . . As soon as we had taken full possession I . . . secured all the property in the place by posting guards at every store-house, magazine, etc. . . . We found three lacs of rupees . . . concealed in a vault . . . covered . . . so . . . that perhaps none but soldiers in pursuit of *plunder* would have discovered it.'

On the 28th the army marched again and by 2 January arrived at Bhurtpore, the next fortress to be attacked. On the 9th a breach was stormed but the attack was repelled with considerable loss. By the 16th they had new siege batteries at work and a new breach had been made by the 21st when another attack was mounted, but this again proved abortive and had to be abandoned with further serious losses. Finally, after nearly a month's further preparation, yet another attack was launched on 20

February, but it too was repelled with considerable loss of life. The following day yet another assault was mounted and Pester and his men were under heavy fire for 'a full hour'. With losses of 180 men and two officers, only John Pester and two other officers were left alive.

By this time their siege cannon were worn out and required replacement, but it was 22 March before one new eighteen-pounder arrived. As Pester pointed out: 'Our troops had now, for five complete months, been exposed to all the hardships and fatigues attending sieges in this fatal climate, constantly distressed by the scorching beams of a vertical sun in the trenches by day and watching with that vigilance necessary . . . by night.'

By 14 April it was generally assumed that negotiations for peace were well under way. Pester noted: 'The weather was getting dreadfully hot and many officers left the Army on sick certificates. I was told by the surgeons that no one's health was more likely to suffer . . . than my own . . . but I made known my determination . . . not to quit the Army on any *earthly consideration*.'

The army next withdrew to Agra in pursuit of the Scindian forces. Although undoubtedly far from well, Pester still had considerable reserves, as is indicated by an entry on 22 April. He was riding out as Brigade Major with a newly arrived Brigadier Brown visiting the piquets and recorded: 'Brigadier Brown was the General Officer today and as he was mounted on an elegant good leaped Arab, and, as . . . he saw I was well mounted . . . was therefore desirous to see what I could do with him. I rode Lassuary and some banks which we had occasion to cross in going our round proved not too high for us, though they at length caused the Brigadier to pull up. Brown was a cavalry officer and had been reckoned a crack rider, but he had never rode a fox chase in a deep, strong country, at least so I suspected.' There spoke the son of the Somerset squire used to hunting in steep-sided valleys and combes at breakneck pace taking it all as it came.

Even so the climate proved too much even for him. On 24 April John Pester noted; 'The sun and wind excessively hot today, and I began to feel the return of the pain in my side. Inglis gave me medicine and blamed me much for having marched with the Army from Bhurtpore.'

This was the end of his campaigning. The army retired to cantonments in June with no further action and John Pester was granted sick leave to return to England where he hoped to see action in Europe. He returned to

India in 1811, having married in the interval. He retired as a Lt-Colonel in 1826 and died, aged 78, in 1856 at Milbrook near Southampton. Apart from sick leave, it was his proud boast that he had never been absent from duty. He remains, in his diaries, a Georgian patriot still breathing fire and ready for action.

CHAPTER TWO

August Schaumann
1778–1840
Deputy Assistant-Commissary: 1804–1814

'The fact that we Englishmen ate so much meat, drank so much wine
and so little water . . . struck the Spaniards with horror and
amazement.'

August Ludolph Friedrich Schaumann was born in Hanover in 1778, the
son of a lawyer. At sixteen he joined the army as a cadet and had risen to
the rank of subaltern by 1799, when he transferred to the postal service
and studied business methods in a school of commerce. He moved to
England in 1803 and worked as a clerk in a shipping company in

Newcastle. Growing bored with this, he transferred to the King's German Legion which was raised almost entirely from Hanoverian Germans who wished to serve in the British army against Napoleon. In 1808 he was enlisted as an assistant Commissary General and sent to Portugal. There he kept a diary of his trials and tribulations between 1808 and 1814 which he subsequently edited for his family in 1827.

His portrait shows him as a bright-eyed young man and his background suggests that he had all the qualifications required for an able commissary, including the ability to organize, an understanding of human nature, and a sound accounting and business sense, as well as a military upbringing. Few commissaries in the army were as well qualified and his considerable energy and genius for survival seem to have made him an ideal choice for such a post. For once the Fates, or an army selection board, seem to have put a round peg in a round hole. After six years of war on the British side it is understandable that he occasionally wrote of 'we English'.

His journal starts dramatically with an account of his landing in Maceira Bay: 'At about ten o'clock on Sunday morning the 28th of August, 1808, we were given the signal to land. . . . I climbed . . . into one of the flat-bottomed boats supplied . . . the men sat four by four in the thwarts, all pressed closely together, with their packs and muskets between their legs. None of the officers was allowed to take more than a valise with him. . . .

'Right and left the coast formed two lofty headlands of rock. . . . Between these . . . lay about 300 yards of sandy beach. Upon this . . . the raging breakers swept in a roaring storm of foam far over the beach. . . .

'With beating hearts we approached the first line of surf. . . . There were twenty or thirty English sailors on the shore, all quite naked, who . . . after many vain efforts . . . succeeded in casting a long rope to us.'

When the boat was hauled up on shore each soldier was carried to dry land on a sailor's back. Schaumann recorded the scene:

'The sun was hot. I undressed and dried myself. The tumult on the shore was interesting. There were soldiers, horses, sailors, officers, both military and naval, shouting and directing the landing; guns, wagons, some of which were being fitted together, mountains of ship's biscuits, haversacks, trusses of hay, barrels of meat and rum, tents, some of which were already put up, and dragoons busy catching and saddling their horses. But the latter could not be mounted, for owing to their long sojourn in the ship . . . they had lost the use of their legs and the moment a trooper mounted . . . the horse . . . dropped his hindquarters to the ground. . . .

'It was wonderful to see the zeal of the British naval and military officers who, stripped to the skin like ordinary gunners and sailors, helped with the landing of the troops, munitions, equipment and guns, ran into the breakers and pulled at the ropes and with their own hands put the guns and the gun carriages together.'

After a night of heavy rain by ten o'clock in the morning Schaumann had dried himself in the sun and shaved and was summoned to the Commissary General where he was enrolled as an assistant, 'with pay at 7s 6d a day and rations and forage for my horse'. He was immediately despatched 'to record and keep count of the sacks and barrels of foodstuffs as they were landed. . . . The whole of the day I had to stand in the boiling heat; the sand was like a furnace . . . and I was almost suffocated. Commissaries-General, officers of high rank, generals and other important people were running about barefooted and in shirt sleeves and everybody was perspiring furiously. The whole of the day we continued to land the 3rd Hussars and the Artillery.'

For a further three days the disembarkation continued, although the wind and seas were rising and on the third day he witnessed a boat containing members of the German Legion capsize, about the fourth or fifth lost in this way.

He described his first sight of a Portuguese bullock cart thus:

'They consisted of rough planks nailed on to a massive pole or shaft. At right angles to the shaft and under the planks two blocks of semi-rounded wood were fixed, having a hole in the centre and through these holes the axle was fitted. It was a live axle fitted firmly to the wheels. As these axles are never greased they make . . . a terrible squeaking and creaking . . . The draught bullocks are very large animals . . . harnessed by means of a wooden yoke, which is fastened behind their horns and attached to the axle by leather straps . . . the wheels are solid, massive and have no spokes. . . . The driver walks alongside with a long pole at the end of which is a spike with which he goads the bullocks on.'

He soon had his first experience of these carts when he was summoned that evening to convoy a hundred carts to Torres Vedras. In the middle of the night he recorded: 'We reached the village of Vimiera . . . which on the 21st . . . had seen the defeat of the French . . . and we went straight across the battlefield, where the stench created by the half-buried corpses of men and horses was appalling. At midnight the rain had penetrated my great cloak and everything I wore right through to my skin and my nankeen breeches hung wet and loose round my thighs. I was almost dead from fatigue and thirst . . . and in the whole of my life I have never cursed as much as I did that night – my throat was quite sore and dry. Anxious to do my duty, for it was the first time I had served the English, I actually wept again and again out of sheer rage and despair; for I fancied that if any carts were missing on the morrow I should be cashiered.'

Eventually he arrived at his destination where he found a Commissary Baxter pleased to see him and reassuring about his having fulfilled his duty. He was then placed in charge of the stores depot for two divisions under Assistant Commissary General Dunmore. He wrote:

'A veritable mountain of salt fish, oats, hay, straw, ship's biscuit, rum and wine had accumulated in one of the large barns of the farm; and on the following morning at four o'clock the quartermasters of seven regiments were . . . standing at the door, together with the servants from General Moore's, Lord Bentinck's and General Hill's staffs, and many others . . . to fetch their rations and fodder.

'The whole day long I had to bake in the sun, reckon up and calculate, weigh and measure, keep accounts and order fresh supplies. I had no assistant and no servant. As a rule our butchers prepared my food for me. . . . In the evening I had to take all my records and a long report to Commissary Dunmore . . . and give details of the state of the stores. . . .

'Very often, however, I had hardly been asleep an hour before some god-forsaken detachment would come along, which had to march off early and I was obliged to turn out to distribute provisions. I also had a number of carts and mules under my charge which I had to lend to regiments drawing rations . . . and this was an additional anxiety and trouble. In short I found that the duties of . . . war commissary are the most laborious in the field.'

Schaumann was undoubtedly the man for such a job, however, being ingenious and unscrupulous about replacing any losses in his stores. For instance, when the division received orders to move on 15 September, he recorded:

'Towards the evening I received another herd of wild bullocks . . . four of which jumped over the five-foot wall of the enclosure and escaped . . . I was very anxious about the escaped bullocks as I held myself responsible for everything that was lost. When therefore we passed a field on our way in which there were twenty bullocks. . . . I then gave my . . . bullock drivers the order to drive our forty bullocks as if by accident among the strange herd and be careful in the end to collect forty-four.'

When they reached their destination 'the four fresh recruits among the bullocks were immediately slaughtered and the marks on their hides obliterated. . . . In a very little while a fellow came running up to us in search of the missing animals, but was obliged to go away disappointed.'

It is clear Schaumann had a natural genius for living off the land entirely suited to his task. He noted that Dunmore and most of the English commissaries fed remarkably badly, but he soon took over their arrangements, stating his views boldly:

'Gentlemen, I declared, if a commissary is expected to starve in the midst of all his stores, then the devil take the whole business. As soon, however, as I took command, we had tea, milk, butter, eggs and beefsteaks in the morning, and marrow soup, roast beef, cauliflower and salad for luncheon. We also had glasses and spoons and I collected a dinner service by borrowing in the neighbourhood. The milk was obtained from our neighbour's goats; our butter was preserved, for fresh butter was not to be had; we obtained our tea and sugar from Lisbon, and the fruit and vegetables were taken from the royal garden.'

In October the army started to march into Spain and eventually Schaumann was appointed commissary to the 32nd Infantry Regiment. Equipped with a large stallion mule with a cracked hoof, which was all he could get in the way of official transport, he set out to join his regiment. He caught up with them at the town of Savacem and reported to their CO, Colonel Hyde. Then he had to get on his way to start his job of provisioning them at the next halt on their march.

After a few days' rest, on 2 November they began their march again in very bad conditions for the rainy season had begun. The road across the San Miguel range was so steep and bad that several ammunition carts were lost, the exhausted bullocks being unable to prevent them falling over the edge.

Eventually he arrived at Villa Vilha where the local mayor swore there was no brandy to be had. Unfortunately the men of the 32nd discovered a supply in a shed and the sergeant major reported almost the whole regiment dead drunk. Schaumann noted:

'The Colonel was furious and solemnly swore he would have the fellows whipped from here to Salamanca. On the following morning a short and summary court martial was held and for a start ten men were flogged so severely with the cat o' nine tails by the drummers that the blood poured from them. Every morning the others will take their turn until the whole regiment has been flogged. . . . From that day forward the regiment became lifeless and insubordinate.'

On 6 November Schaumann reached Castel Branco, where he found himself in good quarters, but the bulk of the regiment remained behind while the ammunition was recovered and fresh bullock carts obtained. It was 15 November before the regiment was on the road again and Schaumann had to move on ahead once more, finally reaching Spain on 22 November.

In one of their earliest billets a corporal accompanying Schaumann had his musket stolen and Schaumann wrote:

'From that moment we regarded all Spaniards as born thieves and false to the core; and subsequent experience never made me repent this hasty judgement.'

On the 30th Schaumann went ahead to Salamanca where he was posted to general commissary duties. Here he had an interview with Brigadier-General Beresford, who was notoriously short-tempered, and it is clear Schaumann was as yet inexperienced in dealing with senior officers. He wrote:

'General Beresford . . . was leaning over a table covered in maps and seemed to be in a very bad temper. He wanted to have a list of my supplies. I gave it to him, and seized the opportunity . . . to ask him whether he would appoint two officers to form a Board of Survey for the inspection of my lame mule with its cloven hoof. . . . He answered me very roughly that he could convene no board for that purpose. Then, in order to put him in a good temper, I took the liberty of pointing to his maps, and of remarking that if he took a number of pins and dipped their heads in red, black, green, or blue sealing wax . . . and then stuck them into the maps he would find that a very clear way of indicating the position of . . . the different corps. . . . He looked me up and down. "I don't want your advice, sir; mind your own business, and take yourself off this instant!" he snorted angrily . . . and I quickly rushed from the room.'

Schaumann was seldom at a loss, however, and his mule was now looking fit and well. He soon managed to sell the beast for a hundred dollars, the cloven hoof concealed with wax, to a miller who thought he had got the better of the bargain.

He was then sent to assist Commissary Mackenzie at Zamora. He recorded:

'Our business here consisted in baking biscuits for which purpose an enormous number of women were employed and many of the bakers' ovens in the town requisitioned. The biscuits when baked were stored in an empty monastery, which towards the end we filled up completely. A number of detachments also passed through the town and we had to give them supplies of victuals. All this gave us plenty to do. . . . The biscuits were . . . really delicious.'

He noted also: 'It is beginning to be very cold and ice is forming on the water in the gutters. . . . I have not failed to see to my own personal welfare. I have bought myself a couple of pistols . . . and had a strong and warm pair of riding breeches made and have also got my mule into the most excellent fettle. He won't leave me in the lurch when we start marching. And we are certain to march now and possibly under the most dreadful conditions.'

On 26 December he wrote: 'The English army has begun its retreat. Everybody is leaving us. We alone are forced to remain behind, for our instructions are that as long as there are stores in the place we are not to move until the French are within a mile of the town.'

On the 28th a messenger arrived and Schaumann recorded: 'We are to leave this place the moment we hear we are no longer safe. Meanwhile we are to dispatch all the biscuit we can to Benevente. Our steeds are therefore standing, day and night, saddled and packed.'

Their final departure was sheer slapstick as recounted by Schaumann:

'A cry arose, "The French are on the bridge!" . . . In great haste we bestrode our steeds and . . . dashed forward at a gallop. . . . At the corner of the street, however, there stood a confounded barrow, which made my horse plunge so violently that I was knocked insensible. I was helped on again and apart from a few bruises was not hurt. . . . Then hardly had we reached the gate of the town than Kearney remembered having left a bag full of gold in the drawer of his table. We therefore halted and with much wailing and gnashing of teeth his poor servant, Juan, a Spaniard, was obliged to go back. However, he soon returned safely with the bag and we went on. Night came on and it began to rain. . . . We halted at Pedreita . . . had a cold meal and laying ourselves in the straw slept peacefully. We had decided to start off again at midnight, but . . . dawn was already breaking when we awoke. While the horses were being saddled we quietly drank our chocolate and then mounted.'

He continued:

'When we reached Ariego, two miles from our night quarters, we overtook twenty-five of the carts we had sent off on the previous day laden with biscuit, or with the sick or English soldiers' wives and we urged the drivers to hurry up . . . a mile further on we were just riding up a hill when we heard some shots in the rear . . . we distinctly saw French chasseurs with shining sabres . . . capturing the whole convoy. . . . We therefore spurred our horses and off we went through St Antonio to Benevente.'

The army was now in full retreat. On the morning of 29 December Schaumann had the task of assisting in a large store depot. He recorded:

'The work consisted partly in helping to distribute rations, and partly in opening cases, boxes and barrels, and laying out their contents – salted meat, biscuits, boots, shirts, collars, stockings, or the most magnificent English woollen blankets. Scarcely had we done this than almost the whole army came along, regiment by regiment, and each man was allowed to take what he liked and as much as he could carry.'

The enemy cavalry then attacked the town and were in turn counter-attacked with over a hundred prisoners taken. Schaumann described these as 'chiefly Poles, Italians and Swiss, also a few Germans'. Then the stores which had not been distributed to the troops were burned in the garden of the monastery where they had been stored. Schaumann noted:

'All the inhabitants of the town rushed to the spot and were regularly invited to snatch what they could. . . . I too was not idle and laying a number of the finest blankets and a quantity of biscuits and rum aside fetched my landlord and made him take the whole lot to his house. . . . The bulk of the army, headquarters and everyone had gone. . . . I then fed my horse, made my amiable host a present of everything I had taken from the stores and lay down to rest a bit, but scarcely had dawn broken when I galloped out of Benevente and away.'

At La Baneza he halted for the night, soaked to the skin by heavy rain. He wrote;

'Here I started a method which kept me fit throughout the retreat. It was as follows: I kept my greatcoat tightly rolled up the whole day on my saddle and let the rain soak me through as much as it liked. Then when I came under shelter I opened my valise and put on my only dry suit of clothes, some woollen socks – for I had thrown all superfluous things away in order to lighten my poor horse's load – and a pair of slippers, and rolling myself in my cloak which had kept dry, I got close to the fire and was able to laugh at the others, whose cloaks had got quite wet with repeated changing, and were no longer any use for a dry outfit. Finally I would hang my wet clothes before the fire, produce some chocolate and cook it with wine and a little pimento and sugar . . . eat a few ship's biscuits and lay myself in my horse blankets on the bare ground and sleep splendidly. On the following morning I would take my dry clothes off and would often put my other clothes on when they were still either wet or damp, for if one moves about in them it does not hurt one.'

The roads were knee-deep in snow and mud and littered with dead bullocks, horses, mules and human corpses. He noted:

'All orderly distribution was at an end. No officer or non-commissioned officer was respected. . . . every soldier took what he liked, everything was plundered, carried away and trampled under foot. . . . Although Villafranca is not small, every corner of it was soon full of men. . . . Fresh troops were always streaming in, the stores depots were also violently raided. . . . In the end Villafranca was literally plundered, and the drunkenness that prevailed . . . led to the most shameful incidents.'

Schaumann by his own account seems to have been the dogsbody of all the chief commissaries during this period. Just as everyone was leaving in the last minutes Commissary Kennedy told him to bring some carts loaded with flour along with him, although the French were at the gates. In the end his sense of self-preservation saw to it that he got out under a hail of bullets, leaving the carts standing.

His description of the road became even more harrowing;

'The road was strewn with dead horses, bloodstained snow, broken carts, scrapped ammunition boxes, cases, spiked guns, dead mules, donkeys and dogs, starved and frozen soldiers, women and children. . . . Discipline became ever more and more relaxed. . . . Every hour the misery of the troops increased.'

Eventually he reached Corunna and found himself a very comfortable billet on 11 January. On the 18th he unexpectedly encountered Colonel Hinde and his old regiment, the 32nd. He begged to be taken under his protection and in a very short time found himself embarked on the *Nimrod* under fire from the French cannon. In addition to the crew and officers they had twenty-two officers and 220 men on board. They then sailed direct for Portsmouth where he was put ashore at last.

On 31 March, 1809, his old chief, Deputy Assistant Commissary General Dunmore, invited him to join another expedition to Portugal, which he accepted with pleasure. By 17 April he was under way on HMS *Indefatigable* and by the 26th he was in the Tagus off Lisbon, rapturizing about the climate after an English winter. He added, however:

'The moment one lands in Lisbon the beautiful vision presented by the white houses as they gleamed afar off in the sunshine is soon horribly dissipated by the badly metalled and steep roads, the heaps of refuse, the dogs, a dead horse covered with flies and in the last stages of decomposition . . . ragged townspeople, whores, the smell of fish fried in oil and broken windows with no shutters.'

On 28 April he recorded: 'Today I landed with all my luggage and took up my quarters at the American Hotel.' He soon received various different orders and noted: 'Nothing but orders, counter-orders and disorder!' Eventually, after various postings were countermanded, on 13 May he was appointed commissary to the 14th and 20th Dragoons and he wrote sourly:

'Mounted on a bad requisitioned mule, without any help, money, or office, and lacking even the means of taking the necessary writing materials and books with me, I was expected not only to overtake two cavalry regiments which had had three days start in pursuit of a fleeing foe, but also to satisfy all their wants and to cross the hills over most appalling roads with fifty bullock carts loaded with provisions and forage!'

At one point he noted:

'I passed a field where the French had bivouacked. All the furniture and even the crockery had been taken from the houses of a neighbouring village and had been brought into the field. The beds and mattresses lay in rows in the mud. The drawers from the various articles of furniture had been used as mangers. Wardrobes had been transformed into bedsteads and roofs for the huts; all the crockery and glass lay in fragments on the ground. The chairs, staircases and window frames had been used partly as fuel for the kitchen fires and partly to feed huge bonfires which had been lighted when the French had withdrawn. . . . In the churches even the graves had not been spared. . . . Altar candlesticks . . . torn vestments, chalices, prayer books and the like mixed up with straw and filth lay all about them.'

Not surprisingly the inhabitants, whenever they had the chance, took their revenge on the French:

'The cruelties perpetrated by the Portuguese hill folk against the French soldiers who fell into their hands are indescribable. In addition to nailing them up alive on barn doors, they had also stripped many of them, emasculated them and then placed their amputated members in the victims' mouths – a ghastly sight!'

His journey was catastrophic. His guide and mule vanished together in the night. After further misadventures it was 17 May before he reported to Colonel Hawker of the 14th Regiment. His duties now started in earnest and on 18 May he acquired some half-wild bullocks for his regiment and some Turkish wheat and corn. On that day he walked thirty-five miles but could find only rye for the regiment which made the horses purge violently. It was clear that the commissary department had failed very badly to supply these front-line troops and Schaumann was left entirely on his own.

On 23 June Schaumann was promoted to Ensign in the 7th battalion of the King's Own German Legion. His duties as Commissary to the 14th and, at this stage, the 16th Dragoons continued satisfactorily as they advanced from Portugal into Spain in pursuit of the retreating French army, but he noted the Spaniards' great reluctance to provide anything without cash payment on the spot. Eventually on 23 July they reached Talavera.

Here he went on a foraging raid across the Tagus with a sergeant, a corporal and twenty dragoons. They were greeted at first with cries of 'Viva Francese' but 'no sooner did the people see the short tails of our mounts – which was then the universal sign by which both French and Spanish recognized English cavalry in the distance – when they cried out shyly "*Viva Inglaterra*". The mayor, or Alcalde, greeted us with the news that the French had not yet been there and at the sight of doubloons he gave orders for his people to bake all night and provide all the bread, cattle and wine they had in stock.'

Schaumann was honest enough to write: 'I made a frightful blunder. . . . I forgot to post sentries and have the place patrolled. . . . After I had settled my business . . . I returned home with my landlord for a meal . . . we suddenly heard . . . cries of "*Français!*" . . . I . . . fled like lightning . . . to mount my horse . . . when forty horsemen tore into the market place – but they wore red uniforms.' They turned out to be a detachment of the

4th Dragoons, with another commissary on the same errand. They had, however, routed a force of French chasseurs also on their way to the town and captured a rival French commissary.

He continued: 'We drank and talked until far into the morning . . . and hardly had the dawn broken, when . . . we returned without mishap to Talavera laden with provisions.'

The next day he was nearly involved in a battle. He wrote:

'Early on the morning of the 27th of July the alarm was given; and, as a battle seemed inevitable, I rode out to watch it. . . . It was a beautiful sight. On the hill to the right was the Spanish army, formed into three tiers, while on the great plain to the left the English army was manoeuvring as if on a parade ground. While all this was in progress a very fine French bivouac, consisting of neatly built huts, full of furniture taken from Talavera and capable of accommodating 20,000 men was set on fire by a detachment of English soldiers, while a number of cornfields in the neighbourhood were also ignited. . . . I was riding about in the midst of it all when General Payne happened to gallop past and . . . sent an aide-de-camp . . . to ask me whether I was aware that the spot on which I was standing was a highly dangerous one. I was informed that the General gave me the friendly advice to go back across the Alberche without delay. Much astonished . . . I rode my horse through the Alberche, grumbling as I went. . . . I had scarcely reached Talavera, when I heard the sound of terrific gun and musketry fire in the direction of the Alberche.'

The day ended in a stalemate and the following day the battle commenced again. Once more the French were repulsed but the British troops appeared exhausted and the Spaniards had deserted them. There were even rumours that the French intended to take the town that night. In the circumstances the commissary staff put their heads together. Schaumann wrote:

'Mr. Myler, Mr. Bailey and myself, therefore, held a council of war and decided that, instead of exposing ourselves to a sudden attack, we should do better to bivouac.'

They had a restless night and woke wet with dew in time to hear reinforcements arriving, who had covered forty-three miles in twenty-two hours, equipped with packs of 50-60 lbs weight, which was good going by any standards. On the Commissary's return to the town they found the retreating Spanish troops had looted their quarters; it was this sort of behaviour by the Spanish, looting the British troops baggage while fleeing from the battle in which the British troops were still engaged, that made Wellington refuse ever again to cooperate with them in battle.

With the end of the battle Schaumann went in search of his regiment which he found on the Alberche and took the quartermaster away to bring back all the limited supplies of food he had been able to find. He noted:

'While on an errand in the town I passed a convent where the wounded were having their limbs amputated and dressed. Never shall I forget the heartrending cries which could be heard coming from the windows . . . while from one of the windows the amputated arms and legs were being flung out upon a small square below. In front of the door lay the wounded, who had been deposited there as fast as they arrived, awaiting their turn. Many of them were already dead.' (He gave the casualties as around 5,000 English and around 8,000 French, which was fairly accurate.)

Because of the Spanish army's failure to hold an important pass the British army was now outflanked and on 4 August was forced to retreat once again. Schaumann began to find General Payne hard to understand and wrote thoughtfully:

'Most Englishmen of high position, particularly when they are serving in a hot climate, are always a little mad.'

Typical of Schaumann's philosophy was his reaction to an order received as he was about to cross the Tagus on the narrow bridge at Arzobispo. He wrote:

'I was seized by Commissary General Dalrymple, who, possibly labouring under the delusion that the English army was going to hold the bridge, asked me in a friendly way if I would ride into the village of Arzobispo on this side of the river. There I would find a few bakers of the commissariat . . . and then I was to requisition all the ovens and see that bread was baked all day! I . . . replied, "Very well, sir!" On reaching the village I found . . . there were a few drivers and bakers . . . but they had no flour, wood or kneading troughs. . . . When I saw how bad things were I quickly decided what to do . . . as soon as it was dark . . . as the French advance guard was expected any moment, we mounted our horses and crossed the bridge . . . as in similar circumstances in Villafranca during Moore's retreat, nobody enquired what had become of me, of the bakers, and of the flour in Arzobispo.'

The retreat was something of a nightmare in extremely hot conditions with very little food or forage available throughout the area. They stopped at Truxillo from 8 to 21 August, when it was decided to march for

33

Portugal. On 1 September he had only just set up in quarters at Villa Vicosa in Portugal where he was rejoicing in good food and conditions when he was sent to Badajoz in Spain. Here he also found good quarters but noted:

'The fact that we Englishmen ate so much meat, drank so much wine and so little water, were constantly on our legs and never slept after the midday meal and yet remained fresh and healthy struck the Spaniards with horror and amazement.'

The army was camped near the notoriously unhealthy Guadiana swamps and he wrote:

'Very soon there was an outbreak of ague and typhus to which thousands of the English army succumbed. . . . Apparently the Spaniards had warned Lord Wellington . . . but he would pay no heed.'

On 20 November, 1809, Schaumann was promoted Acting Assistant Commissary. The General Order reads thus: 'Mr. Showman is appointed an acting Assistant Commissary till His Majesty's pleasure is known.'

In December he was posted to the 16th Light Dragoons as their commissary and joined them at Abrantes on 2 January. He had little to do as there was a large stores depot in the town from which he obtained all his supplies. He was not allowed long here, however, for on 20 January he was moved to the 4th Dragoons in Barquinha. On 17 February they marched to Temtugal. Here there was a great fuss because, although well supplied with maize, the horses remained thin and General Payne insisted that Schaumann provide green forage picked the day before, then bran. Finally, through the local mayor, Schaumann learned that the dragoons were selling the maize in return for bottles of brandy provided by the local women, hence the horses starved. He wasted no time telling General Payne. The result was a general order stating that officers had to see their horses fed and were not to leave until they had finished feeding.

Schaumann made himself very comfortable in Temtugal, but in April, 1810, they marched to Cea. Here he was kept very busy, but he was now saving money on his much higher rate of pay and invested £150 in 4 per cent stock. On 19 July they received orders to march and on the 30th reached Barracal. They were then forced to retreat to Portugal once more, with the French pressing them again, and Wellington introduced a scorched earth policy, ordering the inhabitants to leave their homes.

Schaumann was not too happy when the retreat halted on 26 September and he noted: 'Having reached the ridge of mountains where the

English infantry was bivouacked . . . as far as the eye could see I could discern three columns of a colossal army (75,000 strong) advancing . . . this was the famous French army, the terror of the world. . . . I returned to the camp somewhat downcast . . . for I remembered Corunna . . . drank two or three glasses of grog and then retired a little top-heavy to bed.'

He recorded the battle next day at some length, being particularly impressed by Wellington's ability. He wrote:

'At six o'clock on the morning of September 27th I was awakened by the roar of gunfire. . . . The Portuguese fought with conspicuous courage. . . . They behaved just like English troops. . . . As usual, of course, Lord Wellington displayed extraordinary circumspection, calm, coolness and presence of mind. His orders were communicated in a loud voice and were short and precise.'

Having taught the French a lesson, the following day the retreat continued. Then to his delight Schaumann was transferred from the 4th Dragoons to the 1st German Hussars. He wrote:

'I soon made ready to trot off slyly with my stores and mules when Lord George Somerset to whom the matter had been reported rode up in a towering rage, placed a guard over the carts and compelled me to go off without anything.'

He found the 1st Hussars in front of Mealhada and reported, with his Portuguese assistant, Fereira, to Lt Colonel von Arentschildt. With them he continued the retreat beyond the River Mondego and found numerous refugees, artillery and infantry all mixed together and completely blocking the road. In the crush his muleteers lost several sackfuls of biscuit and similar supplies, but they all assembled outside the town and bivouacked for the night. On 3 October they marched to Leiria which had been looted by the troops, but he recorded:

'Lord Wellington . . . imposed the severest measures . . . indeed the first objects we saw hanging from an olive tree before the gates of the town were the bodies of two soldiers, one English and the other Portuguese.'

On 6 October he reached Rio Mayor. They were now retreating towards the lines of Torres Vedras, starting at Alverca, but like all such retreats it presented a horrific spectacle. He described it thus:

'The retreat . . . from Coimbra to the fortified lines presented a sad spectacle. The roads were littered with smashed cases and boxes, broken wagons and carts, dead horses and exhausted men. Every division was accompanied by a body of refugees as great as itself and rich and poor alike, either walking, or mounted on horses or donkeys, were to be seen all higgledy-piggledy – men and women, young and old, mothers leading children, or carrying them on their backs, nuns who had left their convents, and, quite strange to the world, either wandered about helplessly, beside themselves with fear, looking timidly for their relations, or else, grown bold, linked arms with the soldiers and carried the latters' knapsacks. Monks, priests and invalids – everybody was taking flight. The nearer the procession came to Lisbon, the greater the number of animals belonging to the refugees that fell dead either from fatigue or hunger; and very soon ladies were to be seen wading in torn silk shoes, or barefoot through the mud. Despair was written on all faces.'

On 9 October he spent the night in Villa Franca, still outside the fortified lines around Lisbon, but the following day he reached Alverca:

'Here we obtained the first glimpse of the fortified lines which Lord Wellington had built upon a chain of hills, which seemed to have been destined for this purpose. . . . Running from Alverca to Peniche on the sea they encircled Lisbon completely and had been studded with batteries, mines, trenches and barricades. As far as the eye could see there was nothing but gun embrasures. Earthworks on the hill and barricades made with wine casks, boxes and even trunks filled with earth and stones formed the entrance to Villa Franca; every means of access was blocked. A few 24-pounders frowned darkly upon the road. To the left upon the Tagus a . . . fleet of gunboats manned by English sailors. All garden walls had been thrown down and trenches ran to the very edge of the river. As up in the north we had not heard of these prudent measures . . . our surprise . . . may well be imagined. I sang Lord Wellington's praises.'

Schaumann's regiment was stationed at Ramalhal just outside the lines and he wrote:

'My duty was to clear the ground between us and the enemy of all victuals as quickly and as thoroughly as possible. Accordingly I was given a detachment of hussars from time to time with which I carried out raids. My people followed us with mules and empty sacks. When we reached a village we sent patrols to the left and right of it; then we would go forward, post sentries and proceed to plunder the houses and barns. . . . As a rule the owners had hidden their property badly; everywhere one could see from large damp patches on the walls that something had recently been walled up . . . or from hollow-sounding places in the gardens that things had been buried.'

This does not seem to have been such a dangerous duty as he made out, since there seems to have been a 'gentleman's agreement' between the French and English commissaries, as he described:

'Often the alarm was given that a French foraging party was advancing towards us. But as soon as they ascertained that we were already busy loading up in the place they would halt and patiently wait until we had finished and gone away. Naturally we reciprocated these courtesies if we came to a place already occupied by the French.'

It is difficult after that to believe too strongly in his conclusion: 'If, however, we had met unexpectedly, or on a reconnoitring patrol, we would have fought to the death.'

Finally Massena, the ablest of Napoleon's generals, was forced to retreat since the French had run out of supplies and on 14 November the British army received orders to advance once again. They soon found that the French had left nothing behind them. Schaumann had a lengthy march to catch up with his regiment at Cartaxo and found shelter in a house with some of his Hussars. He recorded:

'I admired their domestic economy. Each of them had a bag hanging from his saddle, in which there was a small metal saucepan together with some ground coffee, chocolate, pepper and salt. . . . All the houses had been plundered; our horses were standing in the ground floor rooms . . . and looking out of the windows. . . . The terrible rains had flooded everything, whole stretches of the country lay under water.'

The cavalry were stationed in the country in front of the lines near Rio Mayor and spent their time harassing the French. The Hussars formed groups of ten or twenty who each kept a small herd of goats or sheep cared for by a Portuguese boy. The officers also each had a boy:

'Humorously called a "rompboy" . . . whose duty it is to go out and steal, from the Portuguese *rompere, robare*, to destroy, to steal . . . and they were smart fellows; for when they were sent out with canteens and sacks they seldom returned with them empty.'

Schaumann appeared conscious of the absurdity of the whole situation and wrote:

'My principal supplies were obtained from . . . stores at Vallada on the Tagus. But, in addition . . . I . . . used to go out diligently robbing with a detachment; for we commissaries were actually ordered to go out in these parts accompanied by armed parties . . . to remove all cattle and corn supplies from the enemy's side of the country and to clear it of all victuals.'

In his foraging expeditions he discovered an estate hidden in the hills where there was a large supply of white wine untouched and he was able not only to supply his own regiment, but also the other cavalry regiments as well. He recorded:

'Before . . . this . . . the hussars in Rio Mayor had supplied their needs from a huge vat of red wine which they found on a farm, but when they reached the bottom of it they discovered to their horror the body of a fully-equipped French soldier. From that day Captain Aly never drank a drop of red wine.'

He spent Christmas at Rio Mayor and noted:

'Before dinner we often rode to a small river where our outpost was stationed. Across this river there was a French bridge which was barricaded. . . . On these occasions the French officers would come down and have a chat. . . . But Lord Wellington who was told about it . . . put a sudden end to this fraternization – and rightly too – by a furious general order.'

Wellington decided to advance as soon as reinforcements arrived from England on 7 March, 1811. The 1st Hussars found the French retreating on the 6th. Then once more the British were pressing the retreating French. Schaumann noted:

'Massena covered his retreat very skilfully. His rearguard was constantly being relieved and consisted of his best troops. . . . Lord Wellington . . . tried . . . to outflank, harass and cut off the French to cause them serious losses and exhaust them. His maxim was never to make a frontal attack and never to give battle so that on the Spanish frontier he might present a fresh and efficient army to his discouraged foe.'

On 17 March a thick mist held them up till midday when they crossed the River Ceira. He noted:

'Here we began to see the appalling consequences of a too hasty flight. . . . The banks were still covered with dead bodies. A number of exhausted donkeys, horses and mules, which had not been able to wade across . . . and which the barbarians had made unfit for use by either hamstringing them, or twisting their necks, were still writhing in the mud half-dead. Among them lay commissariat carts, dead soldiers, women and children, who had died either from want or cold. . . . Over the whole of this ghastly confusion of bodies our cavalry and artillery now proceeded to march without mercy until the whole was churned into a mess of blood and slush. Never during the whole of the war did I again see such a horrible sight. . . . Death and destruction, murder and fire, robbery and rape lay everywhere in the tracks of the enemy . . . the burning villages, hamlets and woods . . . told of the progress of the French. Murdered peasants lay in all directions.'

He began to see the effects of their pursuit: 'On 19 March . . . we found the plain covered with stragglers, dead Frenchmen, arms and baggage. Gradually they were compelled to abandon . . . all the silver, gold, valuables, silks and velvets . . . vestments . . . and crucifixes, which they had plundered from the churches, convents and private houses. . . . Among other things our booty consisted of 1,000 bullocks, cows, goats and sheep, which were handed over to me.'

On 26 March, 1811, Schaumann was promoted Lieutenant in the 7th Battalion of the Legion. He noted this in his journal and the following day recorded:

'I . . . rescued a French officer, by birth a Swiss, who was lying on the heath with a bullet through his leg, and I talked to him for a while. He showed plenty of *sang froid* and taking a pinch of snuff implored me to shoot him dead so that the peasants might not cut his throat. I found a donkey on which he was transported to Sabugal with a few English wounded.'

By 9 April both armies were facing each other on the banks of the Agueda beyond Villa Formosa. The French were now in full retreat and as Schaumann wrote:

'Massena had now returned . . . whence . . . he had set out to conquer Portugal and all he had done had been to devastate the country and lose 30,000 men and a quantity of valuable war material.'

Before they evacuated the fortress of Almeida Schaumann noted: 'The French had hidden live cannon and howitzer shells in the ashpits of all chimneys, baking ovens and fireplaces of the houses and barracks so that the returning inhabitants or troops might be blown to pieces the moment they began to light fires!'

In mid-June they moved into camp near the River Caya and Schaumann did not enjoy it: 'All day long we were infested by snakes, blowflies and other vermin, while our water came from a dirty warm stream known as the River Caya in which the whole army bathed, the cattle went to drink and dirty clothes were washed. At night we were plagued by scorpions, mosquitoes and a piercingly cold wind. . . . The

banks of the Guadiana that flowed not far away were proverbial throughout Spain as plague spots.'

He went down with ague, or malaria, but towards the end of July they
moved from these quarters which had cost something like 4,000 men unfit
for duty, and went to Villa Vicosa. Here in the wholesome air he soon
recovered.

They remained in cantonments until near the end of September when
they were in action again. On 24 October Schaumann was once again
nearly in trouble. The regiment had bivouacked with the rest of the army
in front of Guinaldo. He noted:

'I had established my bivouac in a small field. . . . I went to bed at ten
and must have been asleep a few hours when I awoke. . . . I raised my head
from the pillow and laying my ear to the ground listened. . . . it occurred to
me the sound was not like that of troops entering our area, but . . .
departing . . . orders had been issued . . . to . . . withdraw. . . . I durst on
no account tell the muleteers how critical my situation was for they would
simply have run away with fright and not taken their loads with them. I
therefore woke up my chief muleteer . . . informed him that orders had
just come . . . to retreat forthwith. . . . I hastened the loading of the mules
. . . and about 2. a.m. hurried away. . . . The sun was just rising as I
ascended . . . through a narrow gorge, where I met our General Sir
Stapleton Cotton who . . . said: "Look sharp and get your mules . . . out of
the road. . . . Where have you been all this time? . . . Things will look lively
here in a moment."'

On 7 November the Regiment marched to Covilhao where he had a
further attack of malaria. He applied for sick leave and was posted to Sicily
with the 7th Battalion of the Legion. He went on sick leave in Lisbon
in February, 1812, and with sea bathing his health greatly improved.
He then decided to resign from the 7th Battalion and remain in the
Commissariat. He was accordingly posted to Madrid as quartermaster for
Commissary General Kennedy, but on arriving at Truxillo the
Commissary there was found to be ill and Schaumann was ordered to
take his place. He found the work, though demanding judgement and
accuracy, simple compared with his efforts as a cavalry Commissary.

This was one of the best jobs he ever had as a Commissary, for,
although he held it for only a month before being relieved on 24 October,
he was able to write:

'I had done very well here, for one of the trifling advantages of a depot of this sort was that without being able to reproach myself with the smallest suspicion of bribery, dishonesty, or corruption I was nevertheless able at the end of the short time I had spent here (just over a month) to remit over £700 to England to be invested in 4½ per cent stock.'

On 15 November he was appointed Deputy Assistant Commissary as from 1 September. Then on 27 December he took over as Commissary to the 9th Dragoons in Fronteiras. They were not in action and there was not a great deal to do, but in March, 1813, they were given orders to embark for England and he was ordered to take over the 18th Hussars fresh out from England, a prospect which appalled him as he had had experience of this kind before. His description of Brigadier Sir Colquhoun Grant of his new brigade is explanation enough:

'Every day we commissaries were called before Sir Colquhoun Grant to be reprimanded and to listen to peremptory orders and threats. Our protests and proposals based upon the experience of many years were as good as useless. He imagined that everything would be the same here as in England and thought it exceedingly strange that we should dare to contradict so great a man. . . . Was he not six feet high, and had he not a huge black moustache and black whiskers? Had he not in a dashing fancy hussar uniform carried out the most brilliant cavalry parades on Blackheath? And was he not . . . aide-de-camp, equerry and favourite of the Prince Regent? His whole manner bore the stamp of unbounded pride and crassest ignorance.'

Lord Wellington inspected the brigade, which included the 18th and the 10th Hussars. Schaumann wrote:

'During the manoeuvres poor Colquhoun Grant had to gallop himself almost to death . . . with his brigade adjutant Lieutenant Charles Jones who was also adjutant to the 10th King's Hussars. The latter was a small man with fox-red hair, a red moustache and red whiskers and he also wore a red shako. It was very funny to see him galloping behind the tall black-whiskered general . . . and from that day these two were never spoken of in the brigade except as the black giant and the red dwarf.'

Wellington disliked Prinnie's favourites and Brigadier Sir Colquhoun Grant received a public snub after the parade, which delighted Schaumann. He reported:

'At this parade proud Sir Colquhoun Grant who as the Prince Regent's favourite and equerry expected to be most highly honoured by Lord Wellington . . . was to suffer his first humiliation. . . . Lord Wellington

turned his horse round sharply . . . galloped past Sir Colquhoun shouting
. . . "Grant! If you will dine with me, I dine at six o'clock!" Never shall I
forget Sir Colquhoun Grant's face when he heard this laconic invitation.'

In June, however, they were in action and the brigade distinguished
itself against the French. On 8 June Schaumann noted: 'I rode to the
outposts and asked for four men to help me reconnoitre the villages lying
between us and the enemy for corn, bread and wine.' They were seen by a
French outpost and, he continued, 'a picquet of twelve chasseurs trotted
out towards us. We waited until they reached the foot of the hill and then
retreated slowly. . . . On returning to our posts I met Sir Colquhoun
Grant who for the first time spoke to me in a friendly and affable way and
congratulated me on my courage.'

On 21 June Schaumann witnessed the Battle of Vittoria when the
French were routed and King Joseph, commanding the French Army,
nearly captured. (Joseph had been made King of Spain by his brother,
Napoleon, in 1808.) He spent the night in the town sampling French
wines in the biggest hotel, along with numerous officers. In the morning
he reported:

'Our losses in dead and wounded amounted to about 5,000. . . . The
unmarried ladies belonging to the French army, most of whom were
young good-looking Spanish women dressed in fancy hussar uniforms
and mounted on pretty ponies, or else conveyed in carriages, were first
robbed of their mounts, their carriages and their jewels, then most
ungallantly allowed to go. . . . In some cases, particularly over the
plundering of the wagons carrying the war treasure, our men fought to the
death. No officer dared to interfere. In short more thorough and more
scandalous plundering has never been known.'

The officers of his regiment had their share, as he noted:

'Our Regiment had been ordered at the Battle of Vittoria to hurry
through the town, but . . . it had got drunk and became dispersed. [As a
result of which Wellington put in an adverse report and the officers lost a
year's promotion] Our men were loaded with spoil. . . . The royal kitchen
wagon had been rifled. . . . Every officer . . . got a hermetically sealed tin
which when opened disclosed a wonderful roast joint or fowl in aspic,
perfectly fresh and delicious . . . we enjoyed them immensely.'

He noted later: 'At a . . . jumble sale of Vittoria plunder . . . I purchased
a whole sackful of candlesticks, teapots, silver ingots, plates, knives and
forks for half their proper value.'

On 30 June the brigade returned to Olite, remaining there until 14 September, when they marched to Oscoz in the Basque area of Spain. By 10 November they had reached Sare. There was little work for cavalry in the Pyrenees, until they entered France. Here Wellington took stringent action against looters and Schaumann recorded:

'Pakenham, supported by a powerful guard and the provost marshal, then began to ride up and down our columns like a raving lion. . . . His command, "Let that scoundrel be hanged instantly!" was executed in a twinkling. Over 200 men, chiefly Spaniards and Portuguese, were put to death in this way.'

On 12 November they were on the move again. The weather then turned very wet and cold and Schaumann was kept very busy until January when he fell ill. He wrote:

'On the 15th of January [1814] . . . I was not at all well. Dr. Fiorillo of the 1st Hussars in whom I felt more confidence than the doctor of the 18th Hussars advised me to report myself sick and stay behind in order to consult the French doctors.'

This was really the end of Schaumann's war. He found a very good French doctor and recuperated close to the Pyrenees near Bayonne, but it was May before he was cured. By June he had reported to the Commissary General and had drawn up his accounts. Napoleon had abdicated on 13 March and Louis XVIII had taken over the government on 2 May. The British then were ordered to leave and as, by this time, Schaumann had disposed of his loot and his horses, he sailed from France with his brother Edward on a very overcrowded ship and landed at Portsmouth on 31 July.

He visited London for the Victory celebrations on 3 August, but felt very isolated and alone in the vast crowds. In England perhaps he no longer felt as English as he did amongst the French. By the end of August he and his brother were happily home in Hanover.

August Schaumann lived quietly thereafter in Hanover as a retired officer on half-pay, acting as auditor to an Ecclesiastical Commission. He married and had eight children, dying in 1840 aged 62. He would have been amused that his diaries were published in 1922 by his grandson, Lt Colonel Conrad von Holleufer.

CHAPTER THREE

Lieutenant George Simmons
1785–1858
Diary: 1809–1815

'I have made many friends since I embraced a military life. In my situation I am content and happy, and meeting the enemy never costs me a second thought.'

George Simmons was born in 1785, the eldest of a family of nine sons and three daughters. Initially he studied medicine, and when the threat of invasion by Napoleon seemed very real in 1805 he was commissioned as assistant surgeon in the Royal South Lincolnshire militia which was commanded by Colonel Sibthorpe, MP. He served with the militia for four years and became very friendly with his Colonel during that time.

In 1809 the militia regiment was sent to Hythe where the two battalions of the 95th Rifle Regiment were also stationed, very much depleted after heavy casualties in the disastrous Corunna campaign. Any officer in the militia who could induce a hundred volunteers amongst his men to join the Rifle regiments was granted a commission. George Simmons, forsaking medicine for war, had little difficulty in doing so, since, although only founded nine years previously, the 'Rifle' regiments were already famous for the accuracy of their rifle as opposed to the musket, the old 'Brown Bess' still used by most of the army. They had already made their presence felt on the battlefield and acquired considerable battle honours and fame as part of the famous Light Division which was constantly in action.

Equipped with a warm recommendation from his militia commander to Colonel Beckwith of his new regiment, he embarked with them on 25 May and on 18 June they reached Lisbon. On 3 July he had his first experience of a bivouac in the open at a village called Vallada. He wrote to his parents: 'Halted upon a common: each man took his greatcoat and contentedly lay down; and for the first time in my life I slept very comfortably upon the ground. After sleeping three hours, the bugles sounded.' In his diary, more truthfully, he recorded:

'Hungry, wet and cold, and without any covering, we lay down by the side of the river. I put one hand in my pocket and the other in my bosom, and lay shivering and thinking of the glorious life of a soldier until I fell fast asleep. We fell in at daylight. I found the dew had wet me through, but the sun soon made his appearance and dried me.

'Marched into the town of Santarem. . . . I made my way immediately with many hungry fellows to a *bodega* [inn]. Breakfast was instantly produced, but the quantity of each article did not at all agree with our ideas of a breakfast. . . . I got a billet upon a blacksmith, and found his family very kind. They brought me fruit, wine and cakes but as I do not understand one word of the language properly, everything was done by signs.'

They marched for the Spanish frontier, entering Spain on 20 July. On the 28th they received orders from Wellington to make all speed to join the army in action against the French.

In a letter to his parents he wrote: 'We very soon passed the frontiers of Portugal and entered Spain by forced marches, generally of twenty

English miles by day and sometimes much more, the weather hot and sultry and the roads very bad . . . the villages in general were deserted . . . one entire scene of ruin; some towns were completely burnt to the ground. Even the cornfields (of this year's produce) were generally laid waste by fire wherever the French had been. . . . We daily experienced great hardships from want of a proper supply of bread and food of every kind.'

He noted: 'Arrived early upon the field of battle at Talavera de la Reyna this morning, completing thirty miles during the night, having marched sixty-two English miles in twenty-six hours.'

Despite their forced marches they arrived at the battlefield after the French had been defeated. At the first sight of a battlefield he wrote: 'The horrid sights were beyond anything I could have imagined. Thousands dead and dying in every direction, horses, men, French and English, in whole lines who had cut each other down and I am sorry to say the Spaniards butchering the wounded Frenchmen at every opportunity and stripping them naked.'

The Light Brigade was then sent forward in case the French renewed the action, but they had clearly had enough. The next day they had the unpleasant task of 'collecting the dead bodies and putting them into large heaps mixed with faggots and burning them. The stench from so many dead bodies was volatile and offensive beyond conception as the heat of the weather was very great.'

For the remainder of August they appear to have been on the move. At one point, in charge of the provost guard, he was ordered to pick up all the stragglers and ensure no baggage was left on the road. He noted:

'The only baggage I found was the General's light cart filled with wine and eatables. I tried every means to make the mules draw this load, but without effect. . . . We at last started them, but they set off with great fury. . . . The road happened to be very steep. . . . The cart was dashed to pieces and the mules were also sadly injured. . . . I proceeded . . . to inform the General. . . . He had a party to dinner and was expecting his light cart every moment with its contents in the best possible order. When I related the sad catastrophe he was very nearly furious and directed me to march up the prisoners to their respective regiments, to obtain drummers and . . . to flog the culprits – in fact to become a provost-marshal. . . . I was highly indignant. . . . I went . . . to Colonel Beckwith. . . . He took the responsibility off my shoulders. I heard no more of this business, but this General Officer never forgave me.'

In October they were stationed in a notoriously unhealthy area in the flat country on the borders between Spain and Portugal on the edge of the River Guadiana. Here he contracted typhus and was ill for some weeks. He marched with his regiment, nonetheless, on 12 December and on the 18th he noted:

'Marched to Crato, the officers of the Company, viz. five, billeted upon the house of a priest, who gave us all beds and sold us one of the finest turkeys I ever saw, and also some excellent wine which he partook of. . . . In the morning I felt myself as well as ever and from that moment shook off the villainous effects of disease. The weather cool and refreshing.'

The campaign of 1810 started rather unpromisingly. He recorded on 1 January: 'Began the year rather roughly by a long day's march over bad and mountainous roads to the wretched village of Ponte de Marcella.' On the 17th he noted: 'We have had a heavy fall of snow in which I observed innumerable prints of wolves. I endeavoured to track them, but without success.'

So far he had been fortunate in receiving a gradual initiation into the rigours of warfare and the art of survival on the countryside in adverse conditions, which was an essential feature of this type of warfare. The time was ripe for him to see action at last and here again he was fortunate. He wrote:

'On the 11th [of March] with four companies of Rifle Men, we again occupied this post [Barba del Puerco] having our company posted on piquet near the most formidable passes I ever beheld. The French were also posted opposite us. . . . We remained quietly here until the night of the 19th. . . . The night being dark and stormy with rain . . . completely prevented our advanced sentinels hearing the approach of the enemy. . . . Also from the obscurity of the night it was not possible to see any object . . . only one sentinel fired. . . . However, this gave the alarm and a small party stationed amongst the rocks kept up a fire. . . . In a moment the French were literally scrambling up the rocky ground within ten yards of us. We commenced firing at each other very spiritedly. . . . My friend Lieutenant Mercer, who was putting on his spectacles, received a musket ball through his head and fell dead close to my feet. Several were now falling and the moon for a few minutes shone brightly, then disappeared and again at intervals let us see each other. We profited by this circumstances, as their belts were white and over their greatcoats, so that where they crossed upon the breast, gave a grand mark for our rifles. Our men being in dark dresses, and from their small number obliged to keep close together, the ground also being exceedingly rugged, were all favourable circumstances. We fought in this way for at least half an hour against fearful odds, when Lieutenant-Colonel Beckwith brought up the three reserve companies . . . who soon decided the affair.'

For a quarter of an hour after his friend Mercer's death Simmons had been in complete command, until he was relieved by his Company Commander, Captain Hare. In addition to losing Mercer, they had seventeen men killed and wounded. The French who had numbered something like 500 against his initial 43 had lost over a hundred dead and wounded. The regiment received an official commendation, particularly for the fact that they had driven the enemy back at bayonet point and all concerned were obviously pleased with themselves. He noted in his diary: 'This night gave me a good opinion of myself. I fought alone for some time with fearful odds, my friend dead at my feet. . . . After this night I was considered a soldier fit to face the devil in any shape.'

Writing to his parents in April later that year he gave news of his younger brother Maud, who was also serving in the Peninsular campaign: 'He has been stationed for some time at Portalegre in Portugal, an exceedingly good town, while I have been traversing the country for months, not staying more than a day or two in a place and sleeping in tents or churches. For the last two months we have been stationed so near the enemy we durst not take off our shoes. The weather has all along been very bad, continually raining or snowing. . . . This day I marched four leagues under a continuous torrent of rain. I am now under tolerable shelter, sitting drying my trousers over a fire of wood upon the ground, and am in a very ill-humour, having burnt the leather which encircles the bottoms. I have my jacket off and a blanket round me until my jacket and shirt are dried. I am so much accustomed to get wet I think little about it.'

Despite these brave words there must have been times when the continual soakings were more than just a severe trial. He noted, for instance, on 23 July: 'Spent a jovial evening with Lieutenants Pratt and Beckwith in Almeida. . . . We had scarcely left the town when the rain began to fall in torrents; the thunder and lightning of that night was the most tremendously grand I ever beheld either before or since. . . . The Division, officers and men, had no shelter from this inclement night; as to lying down it was nearly impossible for the water ran in gutters among the rocks. I sat upon a stone like a drowned rat, looking at the heavens and . . .

longing for the morning, which came at last and the rain ceased. Our next consideration was to set the men to work to clean their arms and look after their ammunition.'

It was as well that they did so, for almost immediately the enemy began a determined attack: 'The whole plain in our front was covered with horse and foot advancing towards us. . . . We kept up a very brisk fire . . . as the force kept increasing every moment in our front . . . we were ordered to retire half the company . . . the remainder, under Lieutenant Johnston, still remained fighting. . . . I was with this party. We moved from the field into the road, our men falling all round us, when a body of Hussars . . . got amongst the few remaining Rifle Men and began to sabre them. Several attempted to cut me down, but I avoided their kind intentions by stepping on one side . . . thus I got clear off. A volley was now fired by a party of the 43rd under Captain Wells, which brought several of the Hussars to the ground. In the scuffle I took to my heels and ran to the 43rd, Wells calling out, "Mind that Rifle Man! Do not hit him for heaven's sake." As I was compelled to run into their fire to escape, he seized me by the hand and was delighted . . . at my escape.'

General Crauford, anathema to Simmons, then made a bad blunder as he faithfully recorded: 'General Crauford ordered a number of Rifle Men who had occupied a place that prevented the French from stopping our retreat over the bridge to evacuate it before half the 52nd who were on the right had filed over. The enemy directly brought up their infantry to this hill . . . and kept up a terrible fire. Colonel Beckwith . . . saw this frightful mistake and ordered us to retake the wall and hill instantly, which we did in good style, but suffered severely in men and officers. Lieutenant Harry Smith, Lieutenant Thomas Smith and Lieutenant Pratt were wounded and I was shot through the thigh close to the wall, which caused me to fall with great force. . . . For a few minutes I could not collect my ideas . . . until my eye caught the stream of blood rushing through the hole in my trousers. . . . Captain Napier took off his neckerchief and gave it to a sergeant, who put it round my thigh and twisted it tight with a ramrod to stop the bleeding. The firing was so severe that the sergeant, on finishing the job, fell with a shot through the head. Captain Napier was also about the same time wounded in the side. The Division had now nearly got over the bridge; some men put me in a blanket and carried me off. Our General had placed himself some distance from the fight to observe the enemy's movements. I passed him in the blanket. The General had still in his remembrance the loss of his light cart. He told the men this was no time to be taking away wounded officers. They observed: "This is an officer of ours, and we must see him in safety before we leave him".'

Colonel Arentschildt of the 1st Hussars saw Simmons and thought he was dying. He detailed two troopers to place him on a horse and see him to safety in the church of Alverca where the wounded were lying. A soldier in the 43rd Light Infantry who was dying on a straw palliasse insisted on sharing it with Simmons. Then he was transported in a jolting solid-wheeled bullock cart to the Bishop's house in Pinhel. Here he recorded:

'My trousers and drawers were cut up the side; the latter article of dress was literally glued to my thigh ... the ball had passed through the sartorius muscle and close to the main artery, directly through my thigh, partially injuring the bone. The surgeon who visited me shook his head and looked serious, recommending a tourniquet to be put round my thigh and in case of sudden effusion of blood to stop it by tightening the ligature until assistance was procured.'

He was then put into an English spring waggon with three other lieutenants and because the springs were very strong they were bounced around unmercifully on the rough ground and he found his leg immensely swollen, making his servant turn his ration of bread into a poultice. He himself then dressed the wound of one of his fellow officers. One of the other officers felt unable to go on the next day and they had to leave him, 'as the wounded were obliged to proceed daily to the rear or fall into the hands of the enemy.' The following day Simmons learned that his friend had died that evening.

He was then deserted by the drivers of his bullock cart, who removed their bullocks. Only the care of his faithful servant, Henry Short, who accompanied him, saved his life. However, when Short took over as bullock-driver he overturned the cart and only the fact that Simmons was lying on a straw palliasse which landed on a soft patch of ground saved him from further serious injury or death. Simmons also noticed 'two men with guns ... skulking among the trees and keeping at some distance'. He made his servant load his rifle and kept his drawn sword beside him in case they attempted to steal the bullocks. Eventually with the aid of two British artillerymen who had lost their way they captured one of the Portuguese and forced him to act as driver. With Short using Simmons's sword to threaten the bullock-driver, they eventually reached Mondego.

Thereafter they travelled by boat on the Mondego River which was a great deal more comfortable. In this way they soon reached Coimbra. Here he spent the night in reasonable comfort and the next day continued down river to Figueira. There he was put on board a Royal Naval transport, the *Nestor*. They were taken down the Tagus to the Golden Lion in Lisbon, where he ordered a good dinner and felt a great deal better.

Finding the bill there somewhat steep, he moved to a billet in an empty house in the city where his servant looked after him very well. Within a month, however, he 'removed to Pedroso for the convenience of the sea bathing, my thigh being much better, which enabled me, with crutches, to move about. Lieutenant Harry Smith was also with me. I found great benefit from the sea bathing.'

He remained in Pedroso very comfortably for a further month, but in October decided to return to his regiment along with his brother officer, Lieutenant Harry Smith, 'who had a ball in his leg and was also lame'. They only finally got leave to return to their regiments on the understanding that they marched with a detachment of men from all regiments returning to active service on 7 October. On the 9th he was back with his company and by the 23rd he was in action again, capturing a couple of French soldiers while on piquet duty.

On the 25th he entered a church in Arruda with a friend, Lieutenant Strode. They found an old woman dead near the altar. He wrote: 'I looked round and saw a beautiful slab covered with armorial blazonry; it caught my eye and I said to my friend: "The old woman little thought what good offices an English soldier would perform when she entered the church." "What are they?" says he. "Why, she shall be put under that stone and you must assist." We found a large crowbar and soon finished the business to my satisfaction.'

It was with some gratification that he recorded another mistake on the part of his old enemy General Crauford. He noted on 17 November: 'The enemy showed three battalions of infantry and six squadrons of cavalry as a decoy, the remaining part of Junot's corps being concealed from view. General Crauford fancied that he saw the whole of the rear-guard and made his dispositions to attack them, when Lord Wellington arrived on the ground and stopped the attack, observing, "Are you aware, General, that the whole of Junot's corps is close to the advanced body you now see, amounting to at least 23,000 men, a large portion of which is cavalry?" The attack was, of course abandoned.'

On 18 November he was on forward piquet duty at a bridge over the Rio Mayor and exchanged fire with the French piquets, silencing them very effectively. Despite a very rainy night they were ordered to remain in position, but they made a good fire of olive trees to keep themselves warm. There followed a scene which will probably strike a chord in the memory of anyone who has ever been in action in an advanced position and has suffered visits from senior officers. He recorded with evident relish:

'General Crauford, over his wine, took it into his head that the enemy was moving off and he was anxious to be the first to find it out. He came to the piquet and took three soldiers and walked cautiously along the causeway until the French sentry challenged and fired. The General ordered his men to fire and retire. This . . . created so much alarm in the enemy's camp . . . that they . . . commenced a tremendous fire in every direction for some time. The balls came rattling among the trees and General Crauford was sadly annoyed at being deceived in his conjectures and having caused such an uproar with a great chance of foolishly throwing away his life.'

Unfortunately for Simmons, he had left Lisbon before the wound in his thigh was properly healed and on 19 November he noted: 'Being exposed night and day to very inclement weather my health became very much impaired, but I was in hopes of being able to shake off disease.' On the 21st, after being put in cantonments, he noted: 'I felt very much refreshed from dry clothes and something to eat but my thigh was getting worse and my body sadly out of order.'

On the 23rd he noted simply: 'Symptoms of dysentery.' On the 25th he wrote: 'On outlying piquet. A most dreadful night, which made me so ill I could scarcely crawl.' On the 30th he was forced to leave his regiment and returned to Lisbon by boat where he noted: 'By the greatest good luck, La Tour's Hotel was open and I got a bed there; excessively ill.' He then had great difficulty finding a reasonable billet since most of the people he visited feared he might have an infectious fever. Eventually on 6 December he recorded: 'Had the good luck to get into a comfortable house kept by an old gentleman and his two maiden sisters – the kindest people possible. They nursed me and paid me every necessary attention. I was exceedingly debilitated by continued fever and dysentery. I remained very ill for some days but gradually recovered. . . . Nothing of moment occurred to terminate the year.'

By 16 January he was writing: 'I find the rest and comforts I have been able to procure here have brought me round much sooner than I had any idea of. Shelter from the inclemency of the weather and a warm bed have done wonders. I am now as anxious as ever to return to my regiment.'

By 4 February he was ready to leave Lisbon and return to his regiment. He recorded: 'Took my departure in company with my worthy friend Colonel Beckwith. He has been some time in Lisbon with intermittent fever, but is now restored to health.' By 6 February he was back with his regiment in Colonel Beckwith's company.

By 6 March they received information that the French had withdrawn from Santarem and they re-entered the town. He recorded:

'How different this town now appeared; when I last was in it all was gaiety and happiness, and the shops abounding with every luxury and a smile on everyone's face; but now the houses are torn and dilapidated, and the few miserable inhabitants moving skeletons; the streets strewn with every description of household furniture, half burnt and destroyed, and many streets quite impassable with filth and rubbish, with an occasional man, mule or donkey rotting and corrupting and filling the air with pestilential vapours. . . . Two young ladies had been brutally violated in a house that I entered and were unable to rise from a mattress of straw. On the line of march, comparing notes with other officers, I found that they all had some mournful story to relate of the savage French vandals which had come under their immediate observation. . . . The unfortunate inhabitants that have remained in their villages have the appearance of people who have been kicked out of their graves and reanimated.'

On 9 March he noted: 'Came up with the enemy's rearguard. . . . A large body of cavalry showed itself and infantry in force was halted in rear. An advanced squadron of the 11th French Horse Grenadiers was charged by the 1st German Hussars in pretty style and twelve of them taken. The French had taken two Hussars two days before and it was believed had coolly sabred them. The Germans were so incensed at the report that they were going to put some of these men to death, but . . .were persuaded to desist. One of the enemy was a very handsome man and an Italian. He had a narrow escape as he was on his knees and the sword uplifted to slaughter him when Colonel Gilmore begged him off.'

They were clearly pressing the retreating French hard for he also recorded:

'About forty straggling soldiers fell into our hands on this day's advance and the road was often covered with dead Frenchmen, gun carriages, waggons, and pieces of different military equipment.'

They had brushes with the enemy almost every day during this period and he also had numerous narrow escapes in action. For instance, on 12 March he wrote:

'The enemy took up a position . . . in front of Redhina. . . . After a severe struggle we drove the enemy from all his strongholds and down a steep hill to the bridge. We pushed the fugitives so hard the bridge was completely blocked up, numbers fell over the battlements and others were bayoneted; in fact we entered pell mell with them. . . . Lieutenant Kincaid passed with me through a gap in a hedge. We jumped from it at the same moment that a Portuguese Grenadier who was following received a cannon shot through his body and came tumbling after us . . . seeing the mangled body of a brave fellow so shockingly mutilated in an instant stamps such impressions upon one's mind. . . . Lieutenants Chapman and Robert Beckwith were wounded.'

Simmons's medical knowledge was often in demand and when wounded officers asked him to tell them if it was a mortal wound or not he appears to have given entirely truthful replies. For instance, he noted on 15 March: 'Major Stewart, as many others have done, asked me if he was mortally wounded. I told him he was. He thanked me, and died the day following.'

The advance continued daily, with Simmons chronicling narrow escapes and the wounding and deaths of fellow officers after each attack, as well as atrocities committed on the inhabitants by the retreating French. On 15 March he wrote:

'We passed through Mirando do Corva. . . . The town was almost filled with sick, wounded and dying men, abandoned to their fate, and dead. The rascally French had even plundered this place and committed every sort of wanton atrocity upon the inhabitants and then left many of their helpless countrymen for the infuriated inhabitants to wreak their vengeance upon. Luckily for these poor wretches we followed the French so rapidly that they fell into our hands . . . or they would have been butchered indiscriminately.'

Not far beyond this town they found the French rear-guard drawn up in front of a bridge which had already been destroyed. Wellington was not one to miss an opportunity of this nature. He sent Colonel Beckwith and his regiment forward to attack them, while the rest of the Light Division turned their flank. Simmons recorded:

'The French fought very hard, and some finding resistance to be in vain, threw themselves upon our generosity, but the greater part rushed into the river . . . and there soon found a watery grave. . . . I was quite exhausted and tired and was with about fifteen of the company in the same state when we made a great prize. One of the men found a dozen pots upon a fire. . . . We found the different messes most savoury . . . and complimented the French. . . . The men . . . found several knapsacks. . . . In every packet I observed twenty biscuits nicely rolled up . . . they were to last each man so many days. . . . We had been very ill off for some days for bread, so that some of these proved a great luxury.'

The following day Simmons noted: 'There were a great many mules and donkeys close to the river-side, hamstrung in the hind leg. . . . [It] disgusted us with the barbarous cruelty of the French. To have killed and put them out of their misery at once would have been much better.'

During this steady advance the regiment necessarily had considerable casualties. An action on 3 April when they crossed the steep-sided River Coa resulted in Colonel Beckwith being wounded along with a lieutenant, and another lieutenant killed.

A good deal of marching and counter-marching followed as the French mounted a major counter-offensive, which was effectively repulsed at the Battle of Fuentes de Onõro on 5 May. At the end of a hard-fought day when both sides had had heavy casualties he was on piquet duty opposite the French outposts. He recorded:

'I was on piquet in the lower part of the village, near a stream of water which passed through part of the town. The enemy had a captain's piquet on the opposite side of the little rill. . . . We gave up some badly wounded Frenchmen to the piquet and the officer allowed some of ours to be given up. . . . The remainder of the night was occupied in knocking down many an honest man's garden wall and making a strong breastwork to fire over as soon as the day dawned. . . . Before dawn every man stood to his arms and carefully watched its dawning. The enemy we found, when visible, to be not inclined to fight us.'

In a letter home about this time Simmons made several comments which again will strike a chord with any soldier ever engaged in a long period of close warfare. He wrote: 'Clothes are expensive and bad. My jacket is brown instead of green. Never was seen such a motley group of fellows. I luckily got some French shirts and other articles or I should be nearly naked. If you should ever meet with a good spy-glass, buy it, as I should be glad to pay any price for a good one.'

In his journal on 7 June he recorded recrossing the Coa at the same ford where they had fought on 3 April. He noted: 'I had very different feelings now, coolly and deliberately entering a river after marching some distance with a burning sun over one's head, the perspiration running in streams from every pore. Although I was well used to such movements it was not pleasant, but on the former occasion I took the water as kindly as a water dog, for the French skirmishers were firing in our faces.'

Returning over old battlefields proved a chastening experience:

'We bivouacked in a wood of chestnut trees where several of our brave fellows had been buried and whose bones had been dug up by wolves and were strewn above their graves. A gallant young fellow, Lieutenant and Adjutant M'Diarmid . . . had fallen in fight here. I went to see if his grave had escaped the general disturbance. I found his skull lying at some distance. . . . There was no mistaking it; his hair, when alive, was auburn and very curly. This . . . produced many gloomy reflections. I collected the straggling relics and replaced them and covered them over as the last tribute I could pay him.'

On 7 August he was sent back with forty-five sick men to Castelo Branco and delivered them on the following day to the Commandant who tried to send him with more sick men to Lisbon. He recorded:

'I requested he would allow me to . . . join my regiment . . . as . . . it would soon be actively employed. . . . he said . . . he felt it necessary . . . to send me in another direction. . . . I found it useless to argue . . . but I determined to start back. . . . At one in the morning took "French Leave".'

He left on 10 August and caught up with his regiment on the 16th, noting: 'Colonel Beckwith complimented me for returning and although the Commandant had made a formal complaint . . . I had nothing said to me upon the subject.'

In a letter to his parents he laid down his fatalistic attitude to life as follows:

'I have made many friends since I embraced a military life. In my situation I am content and happy, and meeting the enemy never costs me a second thought. It of course makes one gloomy to see so many fine fellows fall round one, but one day or other we must all go. The difference is very immaterial in the long run whether a bullet or the hand of time does your business. This is my way of moralizing when I go into a fight (which has been very often).'

By this time he had been promoted to 1st Lieutenant following a warm letter of commendation from his Colonel to Lord Wellington. On 29 August he recorded: 'In the evening I was ordered by General Crauford to go forward through a wooded country and by a circuitous route to get upon the road leading to Salamanca, and then, discretionally, to move on for the purpose of finding out when the convoy was likely to leave Salamanca for Ciudad Rodrigo. I had a Corporal and three men of the German Hussars with me. I reconnoitred Tenebron and cautiously entered the place, left it and bivouacked for the night within the woods . . . gained information from a party of Don Julian's guerillas that the convoy had left Salamanca, but was compelled to return.'

Their retreat continued, the Light Division acting as rearguard, and Simmons noted: 'The Light Division parson, Parker, went into a house to make himself comfortable for the night and slept very pleasantly. Some time after daybreak . . . a French Dragoon entered his room. Giving his sword two or three menacing flourishes he asked him for his money. He was followed by others . . . who were apt scholars in imitating a good example; pillage and rapine they glory in. The poor parson found himself stripped of almost everything, and, almost naked, was driven over rugged ground for twenty miles without shoes and then put into a prison amongst a group of others and left to cogitate upon his . . . own stupidity for sliding away . . . unknown to anyone in such critical times.'

It was some time before the enemy convoy moved from Salamanca to herald the French advance and in a letter to his brother Simmons wrote: 'About the 21st of September the convoy left Salamanca. . . . General Marmont . . . had collected . . . 60,000 men with a vast train of field artillery. A very pretty escort . . . You will wonder . . . how the devil he could collect such a force at one given point in so short a time.'

As is often the way with armies engaged in prolonged fighting against each other, Simmons's comments were on occasions quite friendly regarding the behaviour of the French, as for instance during this engagement: '*Johnny's* advanced guard pushed in our cavalry, about a squadron, rather unmannerly which caused us to halt and throw out a few Rifle Men to stop his career. Two or three of the most valorous were knocked off their horses, and the remainder retired to a most respectable distance, where they could amuse themselves by taking long shots – an amusement they are fond of.'

By November he was back at Atalaya, where he caught malaria and noted:

'Had the ague daily, and kept my bed from its debilitating influence. I took bark in very large doses, combined with opium and placed a hot stone on my bosom and two at the soles of my feet as soon as there was the appearance of the cold fit. From treating myself in this way I soon dislodged this insidious enemy from my body and gradually recovered.'

Soon afterwards Simmons wrote to his parents with instructions for outfitting his younger brother Joseph, who was coming out to join his brother Maud, as follows;

'You must procure Joseph a superfine red jacket. . . . The collar and cuffs white Kerseymere, a white Kerseymere waistcoat, two pairs of strong grey trousers, made wide like sailor's trousers, three pairs of strong shoes (one pair short), strong leather gaiters. I have always found them the most preferable as they keep your shoes from slipping off and also prevent sand and gravel getting into your stockings. Three pairs of socks. If you could purchase a sword . . . and can get it cheap, buy it. . . . An old sash also you might procure cheap. . . . He must have a haversack made of dark fustian (not too large), a clasp-knife, fork and spoon; also a tin mug, which will serve him for wine, soup and tea. You may also buy some pasteboard and make a cocked hat, or at least have it cut out in order that he can put it in his baggage with some oil-silk, some broad black ribbon for a cockade, and some broad stuff for a binding. The tailor of the regiment will form it; and gold bullion for each end. His baggage must be as small as possible, as the convenience of carriage is very scarce – three shirts will be enough. He must also have a black leather stock with a buckle, a common rough greatcoat; let it be big enough (any colour, it is of no consequence) . . . He must bring two or three tooth-brushes and three little towels, or any other little thing that may have slipped my memory, which may strike you. His brother is a methodical young rogue and will provide him with many comforts and conveniences as the regiment is always in good quarters, which gives them every opportunity of being comfortable.'

The Light Division and the Rifle regiments in particular, of course, were much more often in action than the line regiments and Simmons's comments were understandable enough. Early in 1812 for instance he recorded:

'January 4th: A stormy cold incessant rain during the day. The Agueda much swollen. Forded it nearly up to the shoulders. The men obliged to put their pouches upon their knapsacks and lay hold of each other to prevent being forced down by the current. Some time elapsed before there was any possibility of getting lodged. Officers, men and all huddled together. Got our men better regulated and had three houses for the company.'

The next major battle in which he was engaged was the storming of Ciudad Rodrigo. The outlying fort of San Francisco had first to be stormed on the 8th. Thereafter Simmons noted: 'Began immediately to break ground and before morning dawned we had commenced our first parallel and completely covered ourselves. The enemy kept up a most tremendous fire all night. I became perfectly familiar with the difference of sound between the two missiles, shot and shell, long before day.'

On the 12th he noted: 'Marched back and resumed our work in the trenches. The weather was keen and it froze sharply. Our poor fellows had to cross the river nearly up to their shoulders and remain in this wet state until they returned to their quarters, some working and some covering the working parties, by firing upon the works of this town.'

On the night of the 14th 'I had charge of a party to carry earth in gabions [wicker baskets] and plant them upon the advanced saps in places where the ground was an entire rock and could not be penetrated. The enemy fired grape and consequently numbers fell to rise no more from the effects of it. I ran the gauntlet here several times and brought gabions of earth, always leaving some of my poor fellows behind when I returned for more and glad enough I was when the Engineer said "We have now sufficient". Returned to quarters in a whole skin.'

In the actual storming of the town of Ciudad Rodrigo he made the mistake of volunteering to take charge of some storming ladders. 'At the impulse of the moment I took with me the men required and followed him [the Brigade Major] to the Engineers' camp, where the ladders were handed to me. I marched with them to General Crauford, who was with the advance. He attacked me in a most ungracious manner. "Why did you bring these short ladders?" "Because I was ordered by the Engineer to do so, General." "Go back, sir, and get others: I am astonished at such stupidity." Of course I went back, but was sadly crestfallen. This is what I deserved for over-zeal. I returned with the ladders.'

He then handed them over to a Portuguese captain and his men with

59

instructions as to what to do with them and returned to his company. Subsequently it seems the Portuguese captain placed the ladders in the wrong place, but as it happened this probably saved Simmons's life for when he and his friend came to the ladders he climbed up them in the darkness disregarding his friend's shout that they were wrongly placed. His friend went the other way and was blown up.

Simmons's battalion formed up on the ramparts. 'Some men brought me wine, ham and eggs. I soon made a hearty meal and washed it down with some good French Burgundy, putting my feet to the fire and enjoyed as calm a sleep as I ever did in my life before for three or four hours.'

Among those killed was Simmons's old *bête noire* General Crauford. His own regiment had barely left the ramparts where they had spent the night when some barrels of gunpowder directly under where they had been blew up and reduced the whole wall to ruins.

'We marched back to our cantonment and met part of the 5th Division coming up to bury the dead and put the works in order as men who have stormed a town are seldom fit for anything but vice and irregularity for some time afterwards if left within its walls. The soldiers were laden with all sorts of things and looked like a moving rag-fair. Some liking their bellies better, had their swords fixed and stuck upon them large chunks of corned beef, ham, pork etc.'

For some time thereafter they were on the move and on 14 March he recorded: 'I had been very unwell and kept my bed for some days. Suddenly, this morning, the order to march came; my servant brought me the news. I instantly jumped out of bed and dressed myself. Dr. Burke, our surgeon, saw me mounting my horse. "What, sir, are you mad? You cannot go in your present state with the Division. I have got a car to send you away with the sick." I thanked him but observed, "I am determined to try." I was exceedingly ill, but during the march I was violently attacked with vomiting, and in a very debilitated state got into a billet with my captain at Portalegre with a padre (clergyman), who gave me some chocolate and a comfortable bed and I was somewhat better the following morning and went with the Division to Arronches. Marched to Elvas and felt myself getting better.'

On 20 March Fort Picurina in front of Badajoz was carried by a storming party and again Simmons had the task of building the first trenches to storm the town. With his marksmen he was then able to keep the guns of the fort silenced during daylight by firing into the embrasures and picking off the gunners.

'A French officer (I suppose a marksman) who hid himself in some long grass, first placed his cocked hat some little distance from him for us to fire at. Several of his men handed him loaded muskets in order that he might fire more frequently. I was leaning half over the trench watching his movements. I observed his head and being exceedingly anxious that the man who was going to fire should see him I directed him to lay his rifle over my left shoulder as a more elevated rest for him. He fired. Through my eagerness I had entirely overlooked his pan, so that it was in close contact with my left ear . . . and the side of my head, which was singed and the ear cut and burnt. . . . We soon put the Frenchman out of that. He left his cocked hat, which remained there until dark, so that we had either killed or wounded him.'

On 6 April the breaches at Badajoz were declared practicable. Simmons wrote: 'My old captain, Major O'Hare, was to lead the storming party. I wanted to go with him, but those senior demanded it as their right. . . . Our storming party was soon hotly engaged . . . the French cannon sweeping the ditches with a most destructive fire. . . . The ditch now, from the place where we entered to near the top of the breaches, was covered with dead and dying soldiers. . . . We were ordered to leave and . . . formed up on the plain.'

To repel the furious attack on the breaches the French had had to withdraw troops from the defence of the castle, which commanded the town and the attack on this was now successful.

'A staff officer rode up and said, "Lord Wellington orders the Light Division to return immediately and attack the breaches." We moved back to this bloody work as if nothing had happened. . . . We entered the ditches and . . . dashed forward to the breaches . . . and we entered without opposition. . . . The prisoners were secured and the place was given up to be plundered and pillaged. . . . I went into a genteel house. The Spaniard told me the French Quartermaster General had lived with him. . . . I sat down and drank a bottle of wine and got some eggs and bacon fried. When the day dawned I went to see the breaches. . . . I saw my poor friend Major O'Hare lying dead . . . just before he marched off to lead the advance he shook me by the hand, saying, "*A Lieutenant-Colonel or cold meat in a few hours.*" Our loss was very severe. . . . The 43rd and 52nd Light Infantry lost about the same number as ourselves. I am only astonished how anyone escaped, but I was not touched in any part of me. . . .

'I returned to the camp and found the soldiers in possession of all sorts of things brought from the town, and crowds of country people bartering with them for clothes and other articles. These two sieges had demoralized the men very much and coercion was necessary on many occasions (with men that had never behaved ill before) and obliged to be resorted to. The men were made to throw away a quantity of things, and to prevent them secreting any of the articles, their packs were examined, and the plunder that had not been made away with was collected into heaps and burnt.'

On 27 May they were reviewed by Lord Wellington. 'Our men's clothing was covered with patches of all colours, and many of the officers' dresses were in little better plight.' Nonetheless the General commented that the troops '*looked well and in fighting order*'.

Now for the first time, as they moved towards the River Douro, they started entering towns in the centre of Spain that had not been fought over and which they had never seen before. On 1 July Simmons wrote: 'Marched . . . to Nova del Rey. . . . I had a good billet and slept upon a comfortable mattress, which was a luxury I had not had for many a day. My usual bed was two blankets stitched together and made into the shape of a sack, into which I crawled and if I rolled about, the clothes never left me until I took a fancy to crawl out again; my pillow a good sod and a smooth stone, and if, before I lay down, I could obtain some wild lavender, which generally was in great plenty, I then had a splendid bed, exhaling the most agreeable perfumes, with the canopy of heaven over one's head. . . . Often before daylight I would have been well soused with rain . . . and in spite of the elements not have been much disturbed. It is astonishing what habit will produce in a man of strong and robust health.'

After reaching the Douro the British army retreated with the French in close attendance. Then on 22 July came the Battle of Salamanca when Marmont was soundly defeated by Wellington. The Light Division was not heavily engaged until about five o'clock when they attacked the French and routed them. Simmons noted one of those strange happenings which occur on battlefields; 'An odd circumstance happened; I saw a partridge running on the ground between the contending lines. I ran, at the impulse of the moment, after it, caught it, and put the bird in my haversack, which afterwards afforded me a savoury supper.' It would, of

course, be a red-legged bird and with muddy ground and the confusion of
the battle its feet and wings were probably clogged with mud, making it
unable to fly, something unlikely to happen to the native grey partridge
Simmons would have known at home.

On 11 August he 'bivouacked in the park of the Escorial. The men of
the Division had only just got off their knapsacks when two large wild
boars were started from a thicket. They were so alarmed at the sight of so
many men that they literally ran directly amongst them, and tumbled over
numbers of them, but after receiving a cut or a stab from a hundred
bayonets or swords, they fell covered with wounds, and in five minutes
their carcases were divided and distributed.'

From the end of August to the end of October the British army
remained close to Madrid and then started another retreat. By 15
November they were retreating from Salamanca once again and Simmons's brother Joseph had joined the regiment in very poor health,
suffering from malaria and dysentery. On the 16th he noted: 'My brother
so ill that I was obliged to give him my cloak to keep him warm. I had given
my mule up to him, so that at every step I was up to the knees in mud and
frequently small rills, which it was necessary during the day's march to
cross, became rivulets from the continued rain. The Light Division, being
the rear-guard upon this retreat, were the first under arms in the morning
and the last in bivouac at night, which was generally some time after dark.'

On 17 November he 'fell in before day. The enemy began to press
us. . . . Numbers of men were left behind and several died. The road was
covered with carcases of all descriptions, and at every deep slough we
found horses, mules, donkeys and bullocks, mingled together, some dead,
others dying, all laden with baggage. It is a most disagreeable sight to a
soldier to see everything going to rack and ruin without being able to
prevent it. About midday the army descended from some very commanding ground and passed the River Huebra at San Munoz. . . .
Our company extended and were the last to retire down the inclined plane
towards the River Huebra, followed at a short distance by the enemy's
skirmishers. The high ground was covered with masses of infantry . . .
also many guns, which played upon us handsomely, which was fun for
them but death for us. . . . On getting through this ford we faced about
and formed columns of battalions. A little way from the ford I found my
brother was absent. Almost distracted I observed him seated some
distance off on the wrong side of the river and the mule close beside him. I

returned through the water with all speed possible and seized hold of him and placed him upon the mule, and uttering a few hearty d--ns brought him safely through under the music of shot and shell. I then made a bugler lead the animal close to me so that I could not lose sight of him.'

His brother was very ill with malaria that night and the mule not much better and Simmons was at his wit's end what to do about them, when he learned the glad news that the French had given up the chase and retired on Salamanca. They marched on the 18th to Ciudad Rodrigo where they 'got fresh provisions in abundance. Bivouacked by the riverside. The night frosty and clear. At daylight, jumped into the Agueda with some of our officers and found myself very comfortable after it, not having had my clothes off, or a clean shirt for some time. The mule that brought my brother through the retreat died this morning.'

They then went into winter quarters and made themselves very comfortable. It is plain that George Simmons' relationship to his brother Joseph was much more that of a father than a brother. He forced him to study and built up his health steadily, so that soon he was two inches taller than his brother and eating 'like a farmer'.

By May, 1813, 5,000 more British troops had arrived as reinforcements and by the end of May the army was advancing across Spain. On 28 May he was close to his brother Maud's regiment, the 34th, and went to see him. 'Remained until dark. Having had an extra glass of wine, I had a better opinion of my knowledge of the road to our encampment than of any other person's, and in consequence I was travelling about the greater part of the night.'

On 18 June they came up with the French: 'We made a sad example of the enemy in a short time and drove *Johnny* . . . to Villa Nana. . . . Our 2nd Brigade took all the enemy's baggage. . . . Our loss was trifling.'

On the 21st came the Battle of Vittoria. Simmons recorded:

'Our third Battalion Rifles was then posted in the village of Villodas, which was directly under the heights. . . . In the afternoon the enemy to our front began to make less opposition and only seemed determined to get out of our clutches as fast as possible, but they had to get over a fine plain which enabled us from time to time to press them confoundedly. Towards evening the road became covered with baggage of every description. . . . We were advancing rapidly. Occasionally a Rifle Man would shoot a horse yoked to a gun. This stopped the rest behind and blocked the way. . . . Night at last . . . afforded a fine opportunity to many to go in quest of plunder. We had fought over twenty miles of ground, I seated myself by a fire with the officers of the company and was fortunate to get part of a ham and some claret which one of the soldiers had taken from a cart belonging to the enemy. In a little time we had a variety of eatables brought by men of the company. I never ate with better relish in my life. I lay down by the fire with a French officer's cloak, which one of the men gave me; he had that day shot its wearer. I awoke at daylight refreshed and in high spirits . . . The French had lost about 10,000 men killed [and] wounded and . . . 151 pieces of cannon.'

They continued to press the French until the end of the month, but General Cloisel successfully evaded them and on the 29th they halted. On the 30th he noted:

'I was sent for wood with a party of men and as it is frequently a scarce article the authorities ordered a house to be given up which we very soon had level with the ground and every bit of wood selected from the rubbish. I was returning to camp when General Picton who commanded the 3rd Division and was coming to his encampment said, "Well, sir, you have got wood enough for yours and my Division. I shall have it divided. Make your men throw it down." Luckily at this moment I espied General Alten, who commanded the Light Division and told him the orders I had received. He was very much annoyed and came up to remonstrate with Picton. . . . I took advantage of it, ordered my men to pick up their loads and be off. Fighting is a very minor part of a soldier's duty . . .'

By this time they were fighting in the Pyrenees, 'marching and counter-marching upon such mountain tracks as would astonish milch goats.' On 31 August Simmons wrote:

'Just before dark I was placed with thirty men upon the side of a mountain. The night now set in very stormy and rainy: we had great difficulty in keeping our fire from going out. I sent some of them to the house of a Spaniard close by and got a large chest. I had it placed on end before the fire and sat in it. I was obliged to be very much upon my guard and the sentries very active, being close to the enemy . . . thunder and lightning were very frequent. By the occasional glare . . . I saw the enemy in full retreat . . . no doubt much alarmed for fear of finding the river not fordable.'

On 7 October they forced the Pass of Vera and for the first time came within sight of France. By 10 November the British army was ready to advance and an attack was made on the French position on the line of the

Nivelle. The attack was successful but in the battle Colonel Barnard was badly wounded and Simmons recorded:

'I was near him when he fell and put my hand into his bosom to feel where the ball had entered. I found his lungs had been wounded as blood in quantities and air issued from the wound; some blood was passing from his mouth also. He in a most collected manner, said, "Do you think I am dying? Did you ever see man so wounded recover?" I observed, "Your wound is a very bad one, but there have been many instances of men recovering from such wounds, and your pulse does not indicate immediate dissolution." "Thank you," he exclaimed. "You give me hope. If any man can recover I know I shall." . . . After all was over Sir James Kemps, who commanded the Brigade, sent for me and said it was his wish as well as all the officers' that I should go to the Colonel and stay with him a few days. . . . I remained with him night and day until every dangerous symptom was subdued and having a good constitution he speedily recovered, and on the 7th of December we rode to headquarters at St. Jean-de-Luz.'

The army then went into winter quarters, but they had established themselves at last on French soil. On 16 February he noted:

'The British army was again put in motion.' The first major battle was at Orthez on 27 February which was decisively won. His next major action was at Tarbes on 20 March when he wrote: 'We were a considerable time driving *Johnny* from all the strong ground . . . but ultimately we succeeded. . . . A Frenchman took a long shot at me; the ball fractured my right knee-pan and knocked me down as if I had been struck with a sledge hammer. . . . My noble servant Henry Short . . . came running to me, and with an oath observed, "You shall not hit him again except through my body," and deliberately placed himself in front of me. Colonel Barnard rode up, jumped off his horse, and showed me the greatest kindness.'

He convalesced at Pau throughout April and returned to Tarbes in May. By 16 May he was visiting his brother Maud in Toulouse. He rejoined his regiment on 20 May by now recovered. This was the end of his campaign and he returned to England and his family, being extremely sick on the channel crossing.

Simmons went on to fight at Waterloo where he was severely wounded, receiving a musket ball which broke two of his ribs near the backbone and went through his liver. Remarkably enough, however, he recovered, although always thereafter forced to wear a corset to enable him to walk or ride. He went on to serve at home until July, 1825, when he accompanied his battalion to Nova Scotia. In 1828 he was promoted Captain after nearly nineteen years' service and he then married. In 1836 he returned to England and in 1846 was promoted to Major on retiring from the service after 36 years. He died in 1858 aged 72.

CHAPTER FOUR

Lieutenant Walter Campbell
1812–1871
Indian Journal: 1829–1831

'We have not a single man fit for duty. . . . Corfield and I are the only two officers not on the sick list and are hard worked accordingly.'

The eldest of his family of two brothers and a sister, Walter Campbell was born in the Highlands at Skipness in Argyllshire. His father died when he was only seven and he and his brothers were brought up in a spartan fashion by their mother. They roamed the hills deer stalking, bare-legged and often as not barefoot, clad only in a kilt and flannel shirt which they

68

allowed to dry on their backs after swimming a river or being drenched while stalking a stag. They rode unbroken highland ponies and roamed the hills freely. In the house, however, their mother demanded a high standard of behaviour and politeness. Thus, they grew up hardy and strong, but civilized in manner and reasonably well-educated, spending six months each year at the Edinburgh High School.

At the age of seventeen Walter Campbell joined the army and soon after he had obtained his lieutenancy his regiment received orders to embark for India. He recorded: 'This news fell like a thunderbolt on many. India was to them a land of hopeless banishment – a living grave – a blank in their existence – a land from whence, if they escaped an early death, they were to return with sallow cheeks, peevish tempers, and ruined constitutions. And such, alas, was the fate of many. But to my romantic imagination it appeared a land of promise – a land of sunshine and perfume – a land of princes, palaces, and pageants.'

His regiment embarked from Chatham on 7 June 1830. By 17 June they had passed Madeira in calm seas with a favourable wind. After rounding the Cape of Good Hope on 16 August they ran into the tail of a hurricane, but survived to reach Ceylon on 12 September. By 16 September they were anchoring off Madras. From the anchorage they disembarked in native boats designed for the purpose.

Once landed, Campbell noted that he and his men were 'beset by hawkers, jugglers, snake-charmers, "coolies" and mendicants, begging for coppers. . . . After standing on the beach for upwards of an hour, braving the fury of a tropical sun and keeping our assailants at bay as well we could, the debarkation of the troops was completed and we were marched up to Marmalong Bridge seven miles from Madras where we found tents pitched for our reception and where we are to remain ten days or a fortnight, to make the necessary preparations to marching up country to Bangalore.'

On 30 September, still at the base camp, he recorded: 'We have now been upwards of ten days under canvas and although we found the heat oppressive for the first few days are becoming quite reconciled to our new way of life. We have been busily engaged since our arrival in procuring tents, horses, servants and camp equipage for our march, and are now ready to start at a moment's notice.

'The following is a list of the principal things required previous to taking the field in India:-

'A Tent – single-poled for a subaltern, and double-poled for a captain or field officer – with two or four bullocks to carry it, according to its size.

'A portable camp-table, chair, and basin-stand.

'A camp-cot, consisting of a light framework of wood, with a rattan bottom, and a thin cotton mattress, on which is packed the table, chair, and other light articles – the whole being carried by two "coolies" on their heads.

'A good horse – or two of them, if you can afford it – with his attendants, or "gorah-wallah", or horse-keeper and a grass-cutter – one of each being required for each horse.

'A sufficient number of bullocks to carry your baggage.

'Two servants; a "dobash", or head man, and a "matey-boy".

'Two "cowrie-baskets", containing a sufficient stock of tea, sugar, coffee, brandy, and wax candles, carried by a "coolie" suspended from the ends of an elastic slip of bamboo.

'A couple of hog-spears – the spear-heads made by "Arnatchelem", at "Salim", and the shafts of male bamboo brought from the "Conkan".

'A hunting knife, also by "Arnatchelem", if possible.

'A hunting cap, strong in proportion to the respect you have for your skull – a thin plate of iron let into the crown is not a bad thing in stony country.

'A good stock of cheroots and plenty of ammunition – it being taken for granted that you are already provided with a gun, a rifle and a telescope.

'Some men, who study their comfort rather than their purse, indulge in a palanquin, a Chinese mat, a tent carpet, and many other little luxuries; but the fewer things of this kind a man hampers himself with the better.'

The troops started their march to Bangalore on 3 October. He recorded an example of the troops' attitude to collecting regimental pets along the way, which indicates that little has changed: 'The road for a great part of the way was bordered by fine old trees, which not only afforded a delightful shade, but swarmed with . . . tropical birds, which afforded constant objects of interest to a novice in the study of natural history. There were plenty of wild monkeys too, which afforded capital sport for the men. . . . On one occasion after a desperate chase of upwards of an hour they succeeded in catching two; one died of the injuries received in taking him, the other was brought here in safety, and is now the pet of the barracks; he wears a red jacket, drinks grog and is learning to smoke tobacco; the sergeant-major, who prides himself not a little on his system of drill, does not despair of teaching him the manual and platoon exercise; and the drum major is quite certain that he will soon be able to beat the tattoo.'

After marching on average a leisurely ten to twelve miles a day they reached Bangalore, 207 miles from Madras, on 26 November. 'We arrived there . . . after an easy march of twenty-two days, including halts.

'Provided the weather is favourable – that is to say neither very wet nor very hot – for either extreme is disagreeable under canvas – I do not know a pleasanter way of spending one's time than in marching by easy stages in India. There is a mixture of wild independence and luxurious living, which is not to be found in any other mode of life, nor in any other country. There is beautiful scenery for the lover of nature – jungles abounding in game, and plains covered with antelope for the sportsman – fruits and flowers for the botanist – beasts and birds for the zoologist – insects, more than sufficient to satisfy the cravings even of a rabid entomologist – constant change of scene for the ennuyee and plenty of fresh air and exercise for the dyspeptic.'

He repeated a story which clearly appealed to his youthful sense of humour regarding the British troops in the fortress at Vellore, which they passed on this march: 'famous . . . for the size and number of alligators with which the ditch round the fort abounds. These ravenous animals are not only unmolested, but encouraged and fed: being considered as they no doubt are, a great addition to the defences of the place. Their formidable jaws, however, have not sufficient terrors to deter some daring spirits among the European troops from crossing the ditch at night. I was told by an officer in the garrision that some "larking" young fellows in his regiment, having discovered that the alligators, being frightened by the discharge of artillery, are in the habit of sinking to the bottom and hiding themselves in the mud for some minutes after the morning and evening guns are fired, avail themselves of the only two auspicious moments in the twenty-four hours, by swimming across the ditch the moment the evening gun is discharged – pushing before them a "chatty" or light earthen jar into which their clothes have been previously stuffed – and after enjoying a night's amusement outside the walls returning in the same manner at gunfire in the morning.'

Compared with John Pester it is clear that Campbell had no burning desire to distinguish himself in battle. His passion was sport and the shooting of tigers, bears, antelopes, deer and other big and small game

71

occupied his mind almost to the exclusion of everything else. Considering his background in the highlands of Scotland this is perhaps entirely understandable. As soon as he could, he obtained leave and arranged to meet his brother up country for a couple of months shooting in the interior.

They had arranged to meet at a small regimental cantonment named Hurryhur. He recorded: 'The regiment quartered here is the 24th Native Infantry. I brought a letter of introduction to one of the officers by whom I have been most hospitably received and comfortably lodged. There are not more than five or six officers present with the regiment and only one lady, the adjutant's wife, who tells me she has not seen the face of a European woman for two years, and complains sadly of the dullness of the place. The country about here is in a very disturbed state. The regiment is ordered to march in a few days to attack a petty rajah who has revolted and fortified himself . . . in a hill fort. . . . The poor adjutant's wife is to be left with an assistant-surgeon and a few invalids to take charge of the cantonment and does not appear at all happy at the prospect.'

Clearly it did not occur to Walter Campbell that he might take part in the action against the rajah. Far more important to his mind was the chance of shooting his first tiger and when he received news that his brother had had to alter his arrangements he arranged to meet at another cantonment called Dharwar. Campbell noted:

'Dharwar: February 24th: I arrived here yesterday without any adventure worthy of remark, except having been stopped during the night by a party of the disaffected natives, who . . . are in a very unsettled state, and have stopped and plundered several travellers of late.

'I was awakened in the middle of the night by feeling the palanquin set down and hearing a scuffle outside. On jumping out with a pistol in each hand, I found myself surrounded by twenty or thirty wild-looking men, armed with sticks, knives and old swords. Two or three of the bearers were lying on the ground with broken heads; and the others . . . were getting unmercifully mauled. Knowing that with my two pistols, besides a rifle and double-barrelled gun, which were also in the palanquin ready loaded, I was more than a match for the poor half-naked wretches who surrounded me, I did not like to shed blood unnecessarily; and, in spite of the urgent entreaties of the bearers to fire, I contented myself with talking in an angry tone, pointing my pistols and making signs to the people to disperse. At first they drew back; but when one of the fellows advanced towards me brandishing a knife, I immediately fired over his head, keeping the other pistol ready to fire into him, if necessary . . . he immediately turned tail, and his companions, uttering a yell of terror, fled in all directions. And so I obtained a signal victory, which was all the more satisfactory for having been bloodless.'

On reaching his destination he noted: 'Dharwar . . . situated more than 3,000 feet above the level of the sea, enjoys a cool and healthy climate . . . the nights are frequently cold enough to render one and even two blankets desirable.

'The country in the immediate vicinity is admirably adapted for sporting, being beautifully diversified with low jungle, open plains and small lakes, and there is no lack of game; but, beyond this, it has nothing to recommend it as an agreeable station. A regiment of native infantry, the collector of the district, four ladies, and a few young civilians, constitute the entire society, and three ladies, out of the four, are anything but young, pretty, or agreeable.

'To anyone, therefore, but an inveterate sportsman, Dharwar must prove a dull station, and even to him the want of female society is a great privation. Although I have not been here more than a month, I already feel this. No one can enjoy the wild excitement of a hunter's life more than I do; but this, instead of weaning me from the more refined pleasures of civilised society, only tends to heighten my enjoyment when I returned to it.'

He was not, however, destined to finish his two months' leave, as he recorded: 'Dharwar, May 24th: . . . I had made arrangements to accompany my brother and Elliot [a senior civilian administrator friend] during their annual official tour through a part of the district abounding with game of all kinds . . . [in a footnote he added enviously; During this excursion in the course of three weeks, (they) bagged thirteen royal tigers, besides panthers, bears, wild hog and deer!] when my bright visions of "shikar" were put to flight by having a long-backed official dispatch thrust under my nose . . . it contained an order to join my company (the light company) which, with the grenadiers and a brigade of twelve-pounders, have been ordered up to reinforce Colonel Evans's division now in the field against the insurgents in the Mysore country. . . . I confess it would have been infinitely more welcome had it arrived a fortnight later.

'My commanding officer, in a private note, is good enough to say I need not join, unless I wish it, before the expiration of my leave. But, much as I admire tiger-hunting, I have been long enough in harness to know that lieutenants in general and the lieutenants of flank companies in particular . . . are expected to prefer man-hunting to all other field sports.'

'My brother . . . has generously made me a present of a favourite Arab colt, named 'Turquoise;' . . . a very promising animal of the purest blood, remarkably fast.'

Next day he noted: 'It was with a heavy heart that I this day bade adieu to Dharwar and my agreeable companions. . . . Rode thirty miles to the village of Inglegy where I overtook my servants and baggage. Much pleased with my little horse – he did the thirty miles at a hand gallop in little more than three hours and came in fresh and playful as a kid. Halted for the night at the travellers' bungalow. These public bungalows, which of late years have been erected by Government at almost every stage along the principal roads prove a great convenience to travellers by doing away with the necessity for carrying tents. . . . The only furniture they contain is a barrack table, two chairs and a rattan couch in each room. To a European eye a large apartment with bare, whitewashed walls, thus scantily furnished, does not present a very inviting appearance. . . . But after a long march, exposed to the sickening glare of an Indian sun, the colder a room looks the better; and the appearance of a savoury dish of curry, flanked by a couple of wax candles, and a bottle of cool claret soon reconciles even a griffin [a newcomer from England] to the naked walls and mud floors and unglazed windows of an Indian bungalow.'

His journal continued with interesting comments on day to day travel: 'May 26th. To Savanoor 14 miles: . . . attempted . . . to sleep on a bare rattan couch infested with bugs, the thermometer standing at about 100° . . . and the atmosphere perfectly alive with . . . mosquitoes. . . . I availed myself of the first peep of dawn to proceed this morning on my journey.'

On 29 May he recorded: 'To Hurryhur fifteen miles. . . . On riding into the cantonment I found that the regiment [the 36th Native Infantry] were in the field and that the garrison consisted of one company, under the command of Captain Babington, by whom, although a perfect stranger to him, I was received with that hearty hospitality so characteristic of Anglo-Indian Society.

'Hurryhur, like all newly established cantonments, is a bare, desolate-looking spot; but has the advantage of being situated in a fine sporting country, the jungles on both sides of the river being well stocked with tigers, bears, wild hog and deer. This I had previously learned from my brother, who has hunted over the ground; and I was astonished to find that my friend the Captain was profoundly ignorant of the fact; neither he nor his brother officers having any taste for hunting large game, and being quite satisfied to keep the pot boiling with a few pea-fowl and partridges.

'We spent a pleasant evening, and, in the course of conversation over a bottle of cool claret, I learned from Captain Babington that our destination is Nugger, or Bednore, a strong hill fort. . . . It appears that a revolt has taken place in the northern parts of Mysore. Our subsidiary force has been called out to aid the Rajah against his rebellious subjects. He and Mr. Cassmajor, the Resident, have hitherto marched triumphant through the country, retaking forts, burning villages and hanging rebels. Bednore, however, has checked their further progress . . . and our two flank companies with a brigade of twelve pounders has been ordered up to reinforce them. The force under Colonel Evans is to assemble the day after tomorrow at Shemoga, a village . . . about fifty-five miles from hence – and we march . . . immediately.'

Captain Babington provided him with a guide and an escort of six native troopers as the country through which he had to march was reputedly 'infested by marauding bands'. Unfortunately all did not go as planned. The following day Walter Campbell recorded:

'May 30th: To Honhully thirty miles; Marched at daybreak. My guide, or guides, – for they relieved each other at every village – being on foot our march was, of necessity, slow and tedious; and we did not reach our halting place until four in the afternoon. The heat was intense and both I and my horse were completely knocked up; neither of us having tasted anything but a draught of muddy water since three o'clock yesterday . . . in those days I carried pistols in my holsters; but I soon learned to turn those useful appendages to better account, by thrusting into one a flask of brandy, and into the other a cold fowl, or tongue, wrapped in paper with a couple of hard biscuits on top of it.'

After arriving at Honhully his escort abandoned him in the bazaar and Campbell was hard put to find anyone who understood his need for food and drink for himself and his horse. Eventually, however, he found a man who understood his broken Hindoostani and provided him with water and curry as well as fodder for his horse. He then settled himself down to sleep in a stable with his saddle as a pillow. He was wakened by a native horseman sent by the major commanding his detachment along with a small party of the Rajah's cavalry as escort.

He noted the next day: 'May 31st: To Shemoga twenty five miles: . . . Having no occasion for a guide today we cantered merrily along and reached Shemoga in time for breakfast.

'My escort consisting of six "sowars" are well mounted on tall, active, native horses and armed with swords and long Mahratta spears. Their bodies are protected by a peculiar sort of defensive armour, formed of pads of quilted cotton, in the form of a back and breast-plate, sufficiently thick to resist a sword cut. . . . The quilted cuirass, although an effectual defence against sword cuts, often proves fatal to the wearer, particularly when wounded, by accidentally taking fire. . . . On a battle-field in India it is no uncommon thing to see wounded wretches writhing in torture; while their cotton armour, accidentally ignited by the flash of a pistol . . . is consuming them in a smouldering fire.

'The country through which we marched this morning bore fearful traces of the sanguinary style of warfare that has been carried on. No quarter to men bearing arms and a dog's death to those taken without them. Every village deserted – many of them reduced to ashes – the fields uncultivated – the cattle running wild – and mangled corpses lying exposed by the roadside, or dangling in clusters from the horizontal branches of the banyan trees. Such sights are at all times revolting, but become doubly so when contrasted with beautiful scenery.'

He described one village in particular: 'It was a lovely spot, situated in a valley surrounded by wooded hills, flanked on one side by a luxuriant mango "tope" and on the other by an extensive tank, or artificial lake, formed by damming the waters of the valley. Countless flocks of wildfowl sported on the surface of the sparkling water. . . . Herds of cattle fast relapsing into their primitive state of wildness were browsing on the green herbage; the morning air was filled with perfume. . . .

'As we approached the air became tainted with the smell of carrion. . . . The mud walls of the huts, roofless and deserted, were blackened by the action of fire; and from the branches of the mango grove hung the bloated corpses of the wretched inhabitants. . . . I counted some fifty of these loathsome objects and remarked that many of them were gray-headed old men, long past the age of bearing arms and beardless boys who had not yet attained it . . . there were neither women nor absolute children among them. Their fate had probably been violation and slavery. . . .

'The bodies, blistered and swollen by the heat of the sun, and mottled with livid spots, indicating an advanced stage of decay, presented a ghastly spectacle. The feet and legs had been gnawed away by jackals and pariah-dogs as high as they could reach; the eyes had been picked from their sockets and the upper parts of the body mangled by the carrion vultures. And flocks of these obscene birds roosted on the branches overhead, or hopped along the ground, so thoroughly gorged as to be incapable of flight.'

He dismissed his escort and caught up with his company that evening just before sunset. He arrived in time to find that cholera had broken out the previous day amongst the force and as he arrived they were in the act of burying one of the best men in his company. In spite of this melancholy sight his return was greeted with roars of laughter from his fellow officers whose nickname for him was the 'Jungle wallah', or wild man of the woods.

He described his own appearance thus: 'Fancy a dust-begrimed figure, with a face tanned to the colour and nearly to the consistency of an old buff jerkin, seated on a handsome Arab horse, but clothed in an old greasy fustian jacket, with brown cord breeches to match; without either neckcloth or waistcoat; his head covered by a hunting-cap of half-dressed buffalo leather; and his legs in long leggings of deer-skin; a belt of leopard-skin buckled round his waist, supporting on one side an ammunition-pouch of the same material, and on the other side a long hunting-knife with a buck-horn handle mounted in silver; a double-barrelled rifle slung at his back and a hog spear grasped in his right hand. Fancy the half-cleaned skull of a wolf protruding its grinning muzzle from under the flap of one holster, and the tail of a rare species of squirrel . . . dangling from the other – and you will have some idea of my personal appearance, and of what the senior subaltern of the Light Company should *not* look like when he rejoins his regiment on service.'

He continued: 'Fortunately for me the major commanding our detachment (a pompous old gentleman and a very martinet to dress) was one of the party who witnessed my arrival. On my first arrival his chin was drawn down into his stiff military stock (an article of dress he never dispensed with even in the hottest weather) and an ominous scowl indicated a coming storm. But mirth is infectious. The merry laughter of my brother subs overcame the gravity of the major. The frown relaxed into a smile, the smile into a hearty laugh, and a kindly shake of the hand satisfied me I had escaped the wigging I so richly deserved.'

Being without tent, baggage or servants he was forced to borrow spare items of uniform from his brother officers and share a tent and the services of a horsekeeper for his Arab mare Turquoise. That evening his friend Captain Babington of the 36th Native Infantry fell sick with cholera.

The following day, 1 June, they marched 12 miles over very rough going. In the evening his friend Babington died and he attended his funeral. A man of his company also died and he had to read the burial service over him as orderly officer of the day. The following day two more men of his company died and he noted that the deaths amongst the native followers were very numerous. As was so often the case in those days, disease was killing far more than the enemy.

On 2 June they marched a further eleven miles through the forests and with his keen eye for wildlife he noted:

'We are now encamped on an extensive "maidan", a plain surrounded on all sides by heavy forest timber. . . . There appears to be an abundance of game. Their tracks are numerous; and about daylight this morning a "sounder" of wild hog, and several deer, crossed our line of march. I had command of the advanced guard, and being as usual attended by my horsekeeper bearing a loaded rifle, I was sorely tempted to take a shot; but my orders being peremptory not to give a false alarm by firing at game, I was reluctantly obliged to hold my hand.'

The next day, 3 June, they marched thirteen miles and he recorded:

'A few miles from camp found the bodies of two Brahmins with their arms pinioned and their throats cut – not a pleasant sight before breakfast. The poor fellows had been sent on the day before . . . with an offer of pardon to such of the insurgents as chose to return to their alliegance . . . a little further on we found the bodies of ten or twelve country-people who had accepted the Resident's offer of pardon, and had been butchered . . . for deserting their cause. This looks as if they have resolved to fight it out.'

The same day on the line of march they found the bodies of some of the insurgents who had been killed by grape-shot while skirmishing on the edge of the jungle and firing at the Resident's column.

'I examined one who had just expired and was still warm. He was shot through the neck and his features were hideously distorted. He had a quantity of ammunition about him and the match used in firing his matchlock was still burning. I took possession of his stock of ammunition to keep as a specimen of native manufacture. The bullets, which appeared to have been cut out in cubes and then hammered into an irregular globular form, were carried in a hollow joint of bamboo, slung over the shoulder, and the powder, which was very coarse, unglazed, and apparently containing an undue proportion of charcoal, was contained in a small cocoa-nut shell, hollowed out. . . . neatly covered with antelope skin, and secured by a wooden stopper.'

On 4 June they only covered ten miles and he noted that the route was little more than a footpath, making it very hard work to move the cannons. The following day was even worse as it rained solidly and they only managed to march six miles with great difficulty 'the ground a perfect sea of mud'.

He recorded with satisfaction:

'Turquoise (my good little arab nag) and I arrange our domestic matters this wise. The weather being too wet for him to sleep out of doors without some covering, I have allowed him to take shelter in my tent and in return, he lends me his rug to sleep on. The tent being very small there is not much room to spare, but he is the most discreet of horses, never thinks of turning or kicking his legs about at night; and so we sleep side by side as comfortable as possible. . . . He is as good as a watch dog, allowing no one to enter the tent without my leave and always wakens me in the morning by pushing me with his nose the moment he hears the bugle sound.'

The following two days the marches were also difficult because of the rains, but, with the help of specially-trained elephants, the bullock trains successfully kept the guns on the move, even though they could not manage more than a few miles each day through the thick jungle.

On 6 June they took a native prisoner and Campbell recorded: 'marched him at the head of the column, with a rope round his neck, to act as guide; having previously informed him that if he led us . . . astray, he would . . . be strung up to the nearest tree. We marched several miles through the jungle, the road becoming more and more difficult . . . till at last it terminated to a mere track. . . . The column was halted and the order given to hang the guide . . . when I, having command of the advance-guard, and having fortunately acquired some knowledge of the native ways in the jungle ventured to suggest that I might be allowed to push ahead a short distance . . . before the sentence was carried into effect. It turned out as I expected. I had not advanced more than a quarter of a mile before I found myself in open ground. It was evident that [he] . . . had been guiding us to the best of his ability, although he had not taken into account the difficulty of dragging guns along the same path through which men could march in single file. So the poor fellow's life was saved; and with a *blessing* from the Colonel, he was . . . allowed to escape into the jungle.'

On the same day Campbell and a friend were near the outskirts of the camp intent on some peaceful sketching of their surroundings when they saw a figure in the jungle and Campbell recorded:

'[It was] . . . one of the enemy's scouts – peeping from behind a tree, and just in the act of raising his matchlock to take a pot shot at us. . . . Not expecting to find either game or enemies so near the camp, I had neglected to bring my rifle and had not even my sword with me; so seeing there was nothing else for it, I picked up a large stone, flung it at his head, and, uttering a savage yell, charged right at him. . . . This . . . was too much for the nerves of poor Blacky, who . . . scuttled down the hill and disappeared in the jungle.'

On 7 June after a march of seven miles Campbell noted: 'We are now within one day's march of Nugger, and tomorrow must decide its fate.' On 8 June, very much as an anti-climax, he recorded:

'Our campaign is ended and Nugger has fallen, almost without resistance. "A very lame and impotent conclusion". No enemy beyond a few skirmishers opposed our advance; a couple of guns placed against the gate blew it open; and as we marched into the fort the enemy marched out at the opposite side. . . . In the evening we strolled down to inspect the fort. . . . The outer walls of the town . . . being built of mud without either ditch or glacis, are not formidable defences; the only part at all strong being the gate at Futtypett, where, by some unaccountable mistake, the first attack was made and our troops repulsed. . . . The fort itself is well built and strongly fortified, but not well armed. We only found some ten or twelve guns . . . so mounted that they could not be traversed and all pointed in the direction of the Futtypett gate, which accounts for our having got in on the opposite side with so little difficulty. They were all loaded nearly to the muzzle with grape-shot, old iron, and other rubbish, and, had they been fired, would probably have burst and done quite as much execution amongst friends as foes. In short I do not feel particularly elated at the result of my first victorious campaign.'

On 9 June Campbell noted a particularly striking instance of how attitudes to death can change under the stress of action or through familiarity. He recorded:

'Poor Paton of the 15th died this morning of cholera. . . . Directly after the fort had been taken, we adjourned to the mess tent for breakfast. This being the only tent pitched, Paton, who had been carried along the line of march in a hospital doolie was brought in and placed in our tent to be sheltered from the sun till the other tents arrived. We were enjoying the good things provided by our excellent mess-man, with the wolfish appetite of hungry subalterns, laughing and joking over our almost bloodless victory, when a gasping gurgling sound attracted my attention to the hospital doolie, which had been deposited in a corner of the tent almost without our observing it. Starting from my seat I pulled aside the canvas covering; and there lay poor Paton insensible and with the death-rattle in his throat. Raising him in my arms, I wiped the cold dew of death from his forehead – supported him for a few minutes until he had drawn his last breath – laid him gently down – dropped the curtains of the doolie – and heaving a sigh for our departed comrade, we all resumed our breakfast as if nothing particular had happened. Death has become too familiar to us to elicit any further remark on such an everyday occurrence.'

On 9 June he noted: 'As there is now a prospect of our remaining here for a few days we have been allowed to make ourselves comfortable by striking our tents and taking up our quarters in the fort.

'The quarters appropriated to us Europeans is an old palace. . . . The men are quartered on the ground floor, and we have taken possession of a large room above . . . divided down the centre by a row of pillars; so that by extending the sides of the tents along them, and between each pillar and the wall, we have divided one half of the room into little stalls, or cells, which we use as sleeping apartments; the other half being left open serves as a mess-room. We have lighted a large fire in the verandah, by which we are drying out our wet things – the first chance we have had for the last week.'

The following morning he claimed to have awoken with the feeling familiar to many soldiers after action that he had 'never enjoyed so comfortable a night'. Despite having only a plank for his bed he had enjoyed the luxury of a dry blanket and not being woken at two a.m. by the fifes and drums for stand-to.

On their return to Bangalore they were immediately back in the normal routine, described by Walter Campbell as 'mounting guard, drilling, paying morning visits, gossiping and flirting with the fair dames and damsels who canter round the race-course, or congregate to listen to the band in the dusk of the evening; a very convenient time by the way for carrying on a flirtation. We have occasionally private theatricals; and about once a month we get up a ball in a handsome assembly-room, erected for the purpose.'

On one such dance evening he was persuaded for a wager of 500 rupees to ride his highly intelligent Arab mare Turquoise into the assembly rooms during the middle of a dance. He rode up the flight of steps to the assembly rooms with no trouble and his mare entered the rooms boldly enough, whereupon the young subalterns started pelting her with their caps, causing her to shy and slip on the polished floor. Fortunately Campbell was a sufficiently skilled rider to turn her round and head her for the doorway. He succeeded in winning his bet but was the first to admit he had been foolhardy and fortunate in the extreme.

He also noted about the same time a comparatively new feature of barrack life: 'It was the custom on Christmas day to give the troops a holiday and a little treat; our men having an extra good dinner with beef and plum pudding served out to them; and the native troops I rather think having a small sum given them to regale themselves withal.'

Not unnaturally such a confirmed sportsman as Campbell succeeded in arranging a further leave for hunting in the Nilgiri hills. On their return from the successful expedition they learned there had been an attempted mutiny amongst the native troops. The ringleader was a havildar of the 9th Native Infantry claiming to be descended from the great Sultan Tippoo, who had opposed the British at the end of the previous century. The whole mutiny had been well planned but the conspirators were given away by a loyal sepoy who pretended to join them but reported the details to his Colonel. The latter was also commandant of the fort at Bangalore and he acted decisively to crush the incipient revolt.

Walter Campbell recorded: 'The conspirators were tried by their own countrymen – a court martial of native officers – and of course found guilty.

'Tippoo and the three other leading men were sentenced to be blown away from guns; fifteen to be shot by musketry and the remainder to be drummed out of the service and transported for life.

'The execution was the most awful and imposing scene I ever witnessed and one not easily forgotten.

'The whole garrison – containing, no doubt, many would-be mutineers – was drawn up so as to form three sides of a square. On the fourth side, which was left open were ranged five guns – twelve pounders – loaded with a double charge of powder. . . .

'Tippoo – a grand looking fellow, upwards of six feet high and about the handsomest man in the Madras army – advanced with the air of a prince, dignified, but not defiant. The other prisoners exhibited an almost equal contempt of death. . . . [They] were placed with their body in contact with the muzzle of the gun, their arms were lashed to the wheels and their legs secured to two tent pegs firmly driven into the ground. Those to be shot by musketry knelt in a row on one side of the guns, with a firing party to each man: and at the word 'Fire' all were despatched at once.'

He recorded in detail: 'The effect of the double-charged guns was tremendous. The body of the victim was blown into fragments, strewing the ground in front of the guns with portions of flesh, which were greedily pounced upon by hosts of kites and vultures. The heads were driven upwards, and the arms flew a hundred yards to the right and left. . . . We remarked as a curious circumstance that Tippoo's head, although blown a hundred feet into the air, fell uninjured – so much so that, being placed on the top of a pile of mangled limbs it was recognised by all who passed and remarked upon as wearing a smiling expression.'

His sporting interlude was quickly forgotten for he was soon recording news of a further move:

'In the month of February we received orders to march from Bangalore to Masulipatam – a march of two months through a country almost depopulated by famine and in which cholera was raging.

'The medical men have taken alarm and predict fearful mortality among the troops if we march by this route.

'Our Commanding Officer forwarded their remonstrances to the Commander-in-Chief requesting that we might be allowed to march to Madras and proceed from thence by sea to Masulipatam.

'Answer – Soldiers have no business to remonstrate. Obey orders, and march according to route.'

On 17 February they accordingly began their march, which, as had been predicted, turned out a disaster. The first cases of cholera occurred on 3 March. Campbell described the death of a sergeant's wife thus:

'I, being the officer on duty, attended the funeral, and read the funeral service over her remains. I shall never forget that scene.

'The uncoffined corpse, hastily sewed up in a sheet . . . the face partially uncovered and dimly visible by the flickering torchlight – the heartrending lamentations of the distracted husband; six young children standing hand in hand, sobbing till their little hearts were ready to burst gazing on their mother with awe-stricken eyes and calling upon her in piteous accents not to leave them; the wailing of the women, and the stifled sobs of the men (for there was not a dry eye among them), formed the most heartrending scene I ever witnessed.

'I managed with difficulty to get through the service with a tolerably firm voice. But when the first spadeful of earth fell upon the naked body, my feelings overcame me. I turned aside and wept like a woman.

'The three men taken ill this morning died in the course of the night. . . . So my journal goes on recording daily deaths and burials.'

He recorded the death of his Colour Sergeant, a burly Irishman named Murphy:

'On the line of march this morning he walked alongside of my horse and entered into conversation with me, making many apologies for the liberty he took in doing so. He said the horror of the scenes he had witnessed for the past few days had so preyed on his mind that he must relieve his feelings by talking to someone who could sympathize with him. He was prepared, he said, to shed his blood and die on the field of battle like a man. But to lie down on the roadside and die like a dog . . . was no death for a soldier; and the idea of it made him shudder.

'I did what I could to cheer the poor fellow. . . . And [he] appeared to be in better spirits. He assisted me to pitch the tents and I went to breakfast.'

Less than an hour later Campbell was approached by another Sergeant who informed him that Sergeant Murphy was dying and wished to speak to him.

'I rushed over immediately to the hospital tent, but so changed was poor Sergeant Murphy, in this short space of time, that I could not recognize him until he was pointed out to me. His ruddy healthy-looking face had collapsed and assumed a livid hue; his eyes had sunk, and his hands were shrivelled up like those of a washerwoman after a hard day's work. He was too far gone to speak; but he squeezed my hand and bestowed upon me a grateful look of thanks; and before the evening gun fired he was underground.'

Campbell noted that the average mortality among the British troops was four or five a day, although, when officer of the rearguard, he found thirteen bodies on one occasion laid out for burial. The native followers literally died in their hundreds. He himself had no fear of infection and noted that it was usually those who took little exercise and feared the infection most who died first.

It was at this time that his early upbringing in the Highlands probably helped him greatly. He wrote:

'Brought up from infancy to contend against heat and cold, hunger and fatigue, a naturally strong constitution and great flow of animal spirits, enables me to bear up under all difficulties; and whatever happens I console myself by thinking it might have been worse. So, notwithstanding the almost overpowering heat – the thermometer at this moment stands at 105° in my tent – I generally take a stroll with my gun, when not on duty, and manage to keep the mess pretty well supplied with game.'

Inevitably he caught cholera, but his strong constitution saw him through. The fort of Masulipatam, however, when they reached it, proved an even worse source of infection, being well known as a plague spot where European troops died like flies. After four months here Campbell recorded:

'August: Our unfortunate regiment is dreadfully cut up. Several officers who managed to struggle through the march . . . now rest in the new cemetery. We have not a single man fit for duty, so that the guards have to be furnished by native troops.

'Corfield and I are the only two officers not on the sick list and are hard-worked accordingly. . . . The main-guard duty is what we dread most; for to the main-guardroom, which overhangs the pestilential ditch, the medical men have traced almost all the fatal cases . . . either of cholera or dysentery.

'The first time I mounted guard I was almost immediately attacked with premonitory symptoms. Something within me suggested port wine as a remedy . . . which I had not tasted since I landed; but on this occasion nature craved for it. I accordingly sent to the mess for a pint bottle . . . which I swallowed at a draught; and so immediate was the relief that I never afterwards mounted guard without repeating the dose. Corfield . . . adopted the same system; and . . . he and I are now the only two officers fit for duty.'

Somehow he survived almost a year in this notoriously unhealthy station. To add to the horror of the situation this was a year of severe famine in the countryside and the inhabitants were dying in their thousands, spreading further disease and pestilence. Then in April he noted:

'I have not written a word in my journal since last October . . . for it would merely have been a record of sickness, death and burrial. Our men continue to die off as rapidly as ever. . . . I have just received a letter from my old friend General Sir John Dalrymple offering me the appointment of aide-de-camp on his staff.'

Despite some pangs of conscience he thankfully accepted this chance of escape from the hell-hole of Masulipatam. It was a further six months before the government decided that the fort was unsuitable for British troops. By that time only fifteen men were left able to parade and the regiment was virtually wiped out, all for nothing.

He was in Madras for a month before joining the General in Trinchinopoly, where he found he had remarkably little to do as a general's aide. His career as aide-de-camp, however, was a short one, lasting only seven months, for the General unexpectedly inherited a large estate on the death of his elder brother. He decided to resign his commission and return home. Walter Campbell applied to go with him, but this was refused on the grounds that he was still fit for Indian service. Fortunately the General was able to insist on having him and he thus escaped what amounted to a death sentence had he had to return to Masulipatam.

Campbell later reached the rank of Colonel before retiring from the army. On his retirement he returned to his family home at Skipness, where the trophies shot during his Indian days hung on his walls along with highland stags. He died there peacefully in 1871.

CHAPTER FIVE

Private Charles Godward
1819–1871
Indian Journal and Letters: 1842 & 1846

'To my great glee found the cook had . . . prepared a fine . . . breakfast with some excellent coffee . . . and after puffing away a mild havana indulged in an hour's soft repose.'

The antecedents and life of Charles Godward are clear enough. Born in Suffolk, at a village called Middleton, near Theberton, in 1819, he was the son of a horseman on a farm, but was apprenticed to a wigmaker in London. To judge by the literacy of his journals and his writing he seems to have had a good schooling at some stage, but perhaps horses were in his blood. Wigmaking he decided was not the life for him and in 1839 at the age of twenty, despite his parents' protests, he joined the 16th Lancers, then in India. He served there until their return in 1846, remaining with the regiment until his discharge in 1855.

Although other private soldiers of this period may have kept diaries of their time in India, Private Charles Godward appears to be unique in that his journal has survived. Thus we have a very clear idea of what service was like in India in the ranks of the European forces in the days when the East India Company was still governing the country. It would seem that he was also something of a character since it appears from his journal that, being stout of build and fond of his food, he was generally known throughout his regiment by both officers and men as 'Tubb'. He was clearly something of a romantic and, it may be inferred from the pages of his diary, an amiable, steady character. Apart from occasional alteration of his somewhat individual punctuation or spelling to make his meaning clearer to the reader, the extracts from his journal are as he wrote them.

The 16th Lancers had already served for nearly 18 years in India and he starts with that familiar plaint of almost every soldier who has spent more than a year or two overseas:

'It was a disappointment . . . felt by all the Regiment . . . after all our hopes . . . of our near return to dear . . . old England to find . . . that yet another campaign was in store for us . . . when at last the orders from the Governor General were read to us, stating that in the present state of the Country he could not deem it expedient to send the 16th Lancers home.'

Godward showed a surprising grasp of the political situation: 'In January, 1843, died the Rajah of Gwalior and Emperor of all the Mahratta States . . . [which] extended over 13,000 miles of the centre of India. On the death of the Maharajah the political opinions were divided. . . . One party was for the young Rajah who was a minor . . . the other refused to acknowledge their existence; this party was the stronger as at their head was . . . (the) Prime Minister of the Mahrattas. . . . We were bound by a treaty made by Lord Mornington, I believe, in 1832 to preserve the direct line.'

He continued: 'The Governor General . . . issued several proclamations for them to lay down their arms . . . this only had the effect of making them worse and they even had the assurance to threaten Delhi. . . . Accordingly on 18 November we left our cantonments. . . .

On the 21st all the Commissariat preparations being complete we had Orders to commence our march.'

He wrote as a carefree bachelor of 24: 'It is at times like this that us single men leave our quarters with merry faces and light hearts, no cares or anxiety on our minds . . . to trouble us, but bright hopes in prospective, so much for single life.'

He made a typically philosophic early entry: '22nd. Marched to Hauper. . . . Confusion and devil of a row before breakfast and all about nothing. Wore off under the soothing influence of the Bobachee [Cook]. Things have not got into their places yet, but a few days will put all to rights.'

He continued somewhat unexpectedly: 'After breakfast myself and comrade (he with sketchbook in hand) took a walk to the town which is of considerable size and the seat of one of the Government breeding studs from which are supplied some excellent horses for the Indian Army. After rambling through the Bazaar without seeing anything particular . . . and noticing a rather curious building at some little distance went to it and found it to be a Hindu Temple rather prettily decorated and not a bad subject for a sketch.'

The presence of two private soldiers was not apparently welcomed and he wrote:

'The two Fakirs, however, who inhabited it did not seem exactly to like admitting Feringhees [Englishmen], but were informed of the object of our visit. They rather complacently allowed us just within the walls that surrounded it. As my comrade proceeded in his sketch of the building the Fakirs seemed delighted with the resemblance it bore to their Sacred Temple and entered very freely into conversation. . . . The Gentleman who seemed to be the Head of the Establishment, before my companion had finished his sketch, told us to take off our shoes, which we did and were conducted by him to the doorway of the Temple, but no further. However, we found ourselves in front of the Idols, three in number which were seated on a sort of altar in a recess at the back . . . and the whole bore a great resemblance to the Altar of a Catholic Chapel, had the idols . . . been changed for a Crucifix. . . . The Fakir who showed them to us wished my companion very much to take a sketch of them, but as it was getting late we were compelled to make our Salaams without complying and make the best of our way home to evening Stable Parade.'

The next day they were on the move again and he noted: 'Galontie

Road: Most infernally dusty, in a wretched humour on account of my horse not walking as is the case with many more just leaving Quarters. Our horses are very fresh, having little or no work lately. A week on the road will bring them to their work.' Riding a fresh horse which is perpetually jogging and refusing to walk out is, of course, a very tiring and irritating business and in the circumstances his comments were restrained.

After a lengthy, dusty and tiring march, on 25 November they reached Khoorja where he noted: 'The country is very fertile and well cultivated abounding in game of all kinds, particularly Pea Fowl which are very easily procured, so much so that with a carbine you are sure of coming home laden with two or three.'

His next entry made this point clear: '26 Nov. It being Sunday we halted, but soldiers like us did not devote much of it to prayer. Quite the reverse as a number of shooting parties were made up, one from my tent, who brought home a splendid assortment of game from which we anticipate a sumptuous repast tomorrow morning.'

The march continued and he noted: '29 Nov: March at six o'clock a most bitter cold morning for this country which is felt most severely by us hot-house plants. The cold, as also the immense number of water fowl that passed over us, plainly indicated that we were nearing the River Jumna but still withal it is very pleasant for without a doubt this is the most splendid part of the country I ever marched through in India and to the sportsman it affords endless amusements for his dog and gun.'

His comments on the march itself are of interest:

'30 Nov: A fine sharp morning so much so that to keep the blood in free circulation we had to use a little more exertion than common to keep ourselves warm. A stranger unacquainted with an Indian Camp would be astonished to see with what speed it can be struck and baggage loaded. It takes us about twenty-five minutes to dress ourselves, roll up our bedding, and strike tents. Our bedding which has to be done up in long bundles well corded up with ropes is carried on camels which beast carries from 12 to 16 beds. Our tentage is carried by Elephant, whose load depends on its size. The larger ones carry from two to three tents complete, except in some cases of punishment when they carry more.'

Their march on the 30th ended within sight of a large town and he noted: 'Inquiring from the natives, we found it was the Sacred City of Bindrebund, situated on the banks of the River Jumna . . . thinking it might be an interesting place to visit myself and comrade as soon as we had had breakfast started across the country towards it, he with his sketch book . . . we were richly rewarded on reaching the banks of the Jumna by the beautiful and varied scene . . . far exceeding our expectations . . . up the River as far as the eye could reach, stood palace on palace and temple on temple, descending with beautiful flights of steps to the water's edge . . . The temptation was quite irresistible to my comrade, who instantly sat down . . . and commenced sketching as fast as pencil could move over the paper. . . . I . . . walked up the river side. . . . On returning my comrade had finished his sketch and the sun was already declining towards the horizon rendering it necessary for us to make the best of our way to camp without seeing the interior of the city which we both had a great wish to do.'

On the following day, 1 December, they marched to Muttra at 6 o'clock and Godward wrote: 'Had the extreme mortification of remaining a full hour after the Regiment on the rear guard to see the whole of the baggage up, which is a very unthankful duty and particular this cold morning; however, the old adage has it patience and perseverance will overcome difficulties and after much trouble got the whole of the baggage off the old camp ground and commenced our march to the river where we were delighted to find a bridge of boats . . . [but] we found the baggage cattle in the greatest confusion. And the bridge completely blocked up with too many trying to cross at one time. In the centre was two camels that had fallen with their load . . . however, some of the guards dismounted and got the loads off the fallen beasts and reloaded them after much trouble, making a free passage for the remainder. When again was a general rush and but for the timely interference of the baggage guard would soon have been stopped again and very probably many accidents might have occurred . . . after this . . . a stop [was] put to any further baggage passing until the tents were over.'

He was particularly intrigued by the reaction of the elephants and recorded: 'At this place they showed the sagacity they are possessed of, which surpasses everything I ever saw. It is really a very interesting sight to see these enormous beasts pass over any temporary place . . . that they doubt the security of, they move with such a slow, sure and measured pace, halting at every step and trying the security of the next with their trunk and foot before they trusted their enormous weight on it.'

He ended this account as follows: 'Arrived in Camp dreadfully fatigued with the long march and working so much at the bridge as also a devilish keen appetite for breakfast, which thanks to a good cook was waiting and very speedily dispatched together with a measure of Companies Rum. After which went very good humouredly to work and helped pitch the Tent and spread down the humble pallet, after which a very refreshing wash in some water from the holy Jumna puffed away a mild Cigar and enjoyed a comfortable hour's repose.'

They remained halted for three days, so on the 4th he decided to make a lengthy excursion to see the sights in the city and described it in detail: 'After partaking of an early breakfast myself and comrade started off on our ramble, which we intended should be a long one and see all worth while in this ancient City. A walk of about a mile brought us within the City gates through a number of long narrow Streets to a large ancient Temple in the centre of the place, now, alas, fallen much into decay. . . . It has been in the days of old a splendid edifice with four tall minarets at the angles.'

With great difficulty they climbed the crumbling stairway of a minaret and admired the view. He continued: 'If the ascent was difficult the descent [was] doubly so for we had on spur boots and the steps being . . . narrow we were in danger every step of coming down head first; however, we once more gained the ground floor fatigued enough. . . . We . . . continued our ramble through the town . . . till the sun was declining beyond the horizon.'

A hint of the romantic nature of the books on which he had been reared is to be had from his comments on the houses: 'The upper stories . . . were very beautiful. The houses generally run 4 or 5 stories high and above the front of each run arched balconies one above the other supported by such slender and delicate pilasters and carving that they seem more like the alabaster work of the genies in the Arabian tales than anything else I can compare them to. The only place I have seen at all resembling it are the fronts of some of the Venetian Palaces, but they are far inferior both in beauty of design and delicacy of architecture. . . . Tired and weary, I reached my tent in the evening and as I smoked a quiet cigar thoughts of home and dear friends came over me.'

On 6 December he wrote: 'A fowling party from my own tent has just returned laden with a fine fat buck, a few partridges and some peafowl.'

On 7 December he noted; 'Near Secundra, at which place stands the tomb of the Emperor Akbar, the elevated top of which was to be seen in the distance, so after a sumptuous breakfast off the game of yesterday started off to walk to this magnificent building . . . and after a walk of about three miles reached the still splendid Mausoleum . . . stumbling over masses of brick, stones, etc., we at last arrived at the noble entrance . . . which is an arch of immense extent, in fact the largest I have ever seen, such a one as would grace Buckingham Palace as a triumphant entry in place of the present insignificant one there. . . . On passing through the arch . . . you enter the botanical garden which surrounds the tomb. It is laid out in the finest style and kept in excellent order. I was delighted on walking round it to find a number of English plants and shrubs flourishing in all their native perfection.'

He described the tomb and his reactions to it in detail:

'The tomb . . . stands in the centre of the garden . . . facing the main gate is the entrance. . . . On entering the door . . . you pass along a narrow passage . . . and . . . find yourself in a large domed hall. The only light . . . is given from an old massive brass lamp . . . which . . . spreads a sort of religious gloom over the spacious vault making it appear much larger than it is. This lamp is attended by an old fakir and according to his account . . . has never been extinguished since the place was built which is two hundred years. At this most remarkable lamp I light a cigar which I puffed away seated on the plain white marble sarcophagus.'

He and his companion then went on the roof to admire the view from there and he continued: 'Before leaving I once more entered the vault . . . and smoked another cigar, and while seated here on the tomb I was surprised to see the numbers of natives who come to do homage to it, all of whom had to take off their shoes before they were allowed to enter.'

He went to visit a Catholic Mission on the way back where children were being taught reading and basic skills, but he found the Missionary unforthcoming: 'A remarkable plain man both in appearance and dress.'

He finished his account of this day's varied excursion thus:

'Arrived in camp somewhat fatigued after our morning's ramble and we had fine keen appetites for dinner, which consisted of fine Pea Fowl, some Partridge and Quail and above all during our absence on this truly gratifying excursion, a few had been very busy in unloading the bags of two sportsmen who had come in with an ample supply of game also a fine fat buck, which was already skinned and dangling from an adjacent tree, the haunches of which are to be served up for tomorrow's dinner.'

On 8 December they marched the eight miles towards Agra, but to Godward's chagrin they did not go through the city so that they could see the Taj Mahal, which he very much wanted to visit, but instead camped about two miles outside. He wrote: 'I was much surprised to find nearly the whole of the Army assembled and from the appearance of the camp at present I should say that it is a full four miles round the front as it forms three sides of a square. . . . On marching in this morning we were met by the commander in chief Sir H. Gough and the whole of his personal staff.'

He then chronicled: '9th December. Halted and had the extreme pleasure of indulging an hour longer in bed this morning, which certainly is a treat. Today an order was issued that a pass would be granted to ten men of each troop daily for the purpose of visiting the city.'

The next day he recorded: '10th December. Halted: Very easy morning's work, nothing but taking the horses out for exercise. Sent in a pass. Went to the city, but the distance being so far I had not time for looking about the place, but I hope on our return I shall have a more favourable opportunity.'

The following day saw the arrival of the Governor-General and he wrote: 'December 11th: Halted: Paraded in Review Order and formed a Guard of Honour for the Governor General Lord Ellenborough. He came this morning . . . to . . . negotiate . . . with the Gwalior government. Escorted his Lordship to his encampment which is in the Taj Mahal garden . . . His excellency the Commander in Chief and his staff met his Lordship on his entry into the city, the both staff forming an immense train and such an assemblage of cocked hats are not to be seen every day.'

The next day, 12 December, he recorded: 'Halted . . . news that the Gwalior Army are making . . . preparations for open war and talk of beating us back . . . and taking this city . . . and making us beat a retreat to Calcutta, poor ignoramuses.'

On 13 December he noted: 'Halted. Paraded for Brigade exercises preparatory to a Review tomorrow by His Excellency the Commander in Chief. . . . News arrived of the rapid progress of the other wing of the army which assembled in Cawnpore. Under Major-General Grey this wing of the army is nearing Gwalior fast and enters the opposite point to us . . . This movement of the army marching in different routes will I think much surprise our foes.

'14th December; Halted: According to yesterday's orders the Commander in Chief inspected the Brigade and was much delighted at the fine military appearance of the Lancers, which he expressed in very warm terms, much to the regiment's gratification. Orders are issued to start our march tomorrow.'

Detailed for special duties on the march, Godward had a bad day. He wrote:

'15th December: The Brigade commenced their march this morning at six o'clock but myself being on the Hospital Guard commenced before 3 under the direction of a guide who was anything but that to us, for on marching till sunrise had the extreme felicity of finding ourselves in the 1st Infantry Brigade's encampment, which moved this morning on a different route to us. On making enquiries of some persons in the camp as also the natives of the village found to my mortification that I had come a full 12 miles out of my road which so exasperated my feelings that I verily believe had I got at the guide who had led me astray I certainly would have shot him, but the rascal had made good his escape. . . . However, it was necessary to put a good face on a bad job, but I was not the only one astray for numbers followed the camels under our charge thinking as we had a guide of course we were on the right road. Amongst these were several of those useful individuals and promoters of the peace, the cooks, whose absence in the camp would be the cause of many . . . wry faces amongst the Regiment.'

They pressed several different natives into service as guides, although none of them seem to have been much use. However, in the end they arrived at their destination and he concluded:

'At last arrived safe in camp it being ½ past 10; dreadfully fatigued from having been in the saddle from shortly after 2 o'clock, but after a good wash felt much refreshed and to my great glee found the cook had arrived and already had prepared a fine substantial breakfast with some excellent coffee which was speedily dispatched and after puffing away a mild havana indulged in an hour's soft repose.'

The following day he merely noted:

'16th December: Marched at 6 o'clock: road very bad but the country very fertile and abounding in game and affording an ample supply.'

The next day the grouses started:

'17th December: Marched at the usual hour. Our road is if anything worse than yesterday and having 2 troops of Horse Artillery preceding us detains the Regiment much longer on the road than they otherwise would be, which makes the morning's march very tedious so much so that most of us arrive in camp in the worst of humours, in fact quite quarrelsome.

95

This morning in particular the tent was pitched after much wrangling and many disputes, but the ever soothing influence, the breakfast, put a stop to all these petty squabbles.'

Clearly the artillery were a source of trouble, for he followed this with:

'18th December . . . the road much the same as yesterday and interspersed with some very awkward looking ravines over which we have great difficulty in getting the guns. The country begins to assume a different appearance to what we have been travelling through as low hills begin to show themselves. In front of our present camp is a good height on top of which is a large tomb over the remains of a former Rajah. . . . The ground we are encamped on is miserable, being nothing but red mud which is very unpleasant to walk in, much more sleep on, our horses are continually drawing the pegs they are picqueted to and many running mad through the camp, but we expect to halt here one or more days. There is not the least doubt that we shall shift further back, which is much better ground.'

The next day he was proved right:

'19th December: Halted and, as I had anticipated yesterday, we shifted our camp about ¼ of a mile to the rear on most excellent ground. . . . The Rajah of this place is a complete sporting character . . . keeping a very extensive establishment, a fine pack of dogs and a most splendid stud of horses among which are some of the most graceful and beautiful Arabs I ever saw. There are two very extensive palaces . . . most splendid and furnished in the best English style, some most excellent English furniture and hung with all kinds of pictures, while the adjoining apartments are purely eastern. . . . At the old Palace he keeps a very extensive menagerie of wild beasts near to which was a place stocked with a very choice collection of birds . . . and the greatest variety of parrots I ever saw. . . . On leaving the menagerie . . . walk through the palace yard . . . returned to camp much fatigued.'

The anticipated visit by the Rajah was postponed until the next day, as Godward recorded:

'20th December: Today instead of yesterday the Rajah paid his visit of ceremony. . . . Attended by a numerous staff of followers all very gaudily dressed. . . . Altogether it was rather a shiny party, consisting of elephants, horses and camels, the clothes of the former being beautiful crimson velvet embroidered with gold and silver on a most massive style while the proud and graceful Arabs . . . were literally covered with massive gold and silver ornaments. . . . But the most conspicuous object in this pageantry and surprised us all the most was a town-built carriage drawn by four beautiful horses harnessed the same as in England. This, I found, was presented to the Rajah by Lord Aukland (late Governor General). . . . Tonight orders are issued to proceed on our march . . . to Gwalior at ½ past 7 tomorrow.

'21st December: Marched this morning according to yesterday's orders through a very rugged country interspersed with deep ravines. Altogether the most wilderness looking place I have seen since I left Meerut. This sort of country continued to the camp which is pitched on the left bank of the River Chumble . . . The opposite bank of the River is in places very high and running perpendicular down to the water . . . from the very rugged appearance of the whole I should say that it was a very great oversight on the part of the Gwaliors not marching to this place as . . . a few batteries on the opposite side would prevent us crossing. . . . This part of the country is swarming with game of all kinds and deer running about in all directions. In fact there are continued uproars in camp with different parties hunting them as they keep running through. While standing to see the horses, forage served out this morning saw two beautiful bucks knocked down with sticks.'

On 22 December he noted: 'Commenced to move long before daylight to get the tents and baggage packed in good time for fording the river, thinking from the immense quantity of baggage that had to pass over, there would be great confusion. . . . The Infantry who passed over first was at the ford by 6 o'clock where they had to ford, to do which they had to pull off their trowsers the water in parts being full four feet deep, which was anything but pleasant this cold morning. However, they reached the opposite side in safety. Following close to them was the Artillery. . . . The Cavalry . . . passed over without any casualties except a few wet legs particular those who had low horses.'

From his description the organization was deplorable: 'As no baggage was allowed in front of the column that which had crossed was detained while that waiting was jammed together in one mass each fighting one against the other to gain the ford first. So what with the continual roar of the camels and other beasts of burden, the unintelligable jaw of the drivers, together with many hearty curses from the baggage guard, [it] fully reminded one of . . . the confusion of Babel.

'On our reaching the opposite bank had to wait a full hour for the Artillery, who previous to fording had to take all the ammunition boxes off the waggons to keep them dry and send them over in boats and reload them, which being done again resumed our march, the road running for about 3 miles up a deep ravine. . . . We then came upon a more level country which continued to our present camp in front of which runs a deep nullah with a fine supply of water.'

On 23 December they were halted for several days to bring up the whole army. Godward wrote:

'Strict orders are issued today for strong guards and picquets to be thrown out across the front. . . . Those on the right flank of the camp have orders to keep a very vigilant watch on the village of Sabourie as it is strongly suspected that the inhabitants are in communication with the enemy. Our native spies came in today bringing intelligence that the enemy are all encamped outside the fort and part have marched en route to meet us, as also a party having moved off to meet the Cawnpore Division.'

On Christmas Eve Godward learned that he would be on outlying picquet duty on Christmas Day and had an acute attack of homesickness, as apparently did most of his companions.

'All the tent crew appear to be in the dumps, or more or less low-spirited; as for myself I don't know the day I was so miserable and wretched . . . when I think of the many happy Christmas Eves I have spent in dear old England . . . it still makes me more so, but never mind, I hope to enjoy many more amongst those dear friends and relations . . . as I now sit squatted on the ground writing these lines from a poor but sufficient light . . . I cannot but hear the different conversations of the men around, all of whom are endeavouring to draw pictures of home and the many happy parties assembled round the cheerful fire, while the . . . carol graces the festive board at which so many absent friends will be pledged.'

His Christmas Day was among the most military he had experienced for some time. He wrote:

'25th. "A Merry Christmas to you, Tubb" was the first salutation on awaking from another uncomfortable night's rest as bright visions of home disturbed my repose after my serious thoughts of last night. "Thank you," was my reply, "but I fear there is every prospect of its being anything but a merry one." Struck tents, packed the baggage and had the camels loaded before 5 o'clock. Took up our post long before sunrise in rear of the village of Sabourie and detached a small party in front whose duty was to keep a very vigilant watch on the Bombay road.'

While describing the day he also aired a well-worn grouse: 'Dismounted and picqueted our horses with an order that neither man nor horse to be unaccoutred during this tour of duty in case of a surprise, which was not at all likely. . . . I don't know of any situation so uncomfortable as on outlying duty, when we have to keep buttoned up in full dress the whole four and twenty hours, not allowed under penalty of punishment to take so much as a stock off. At 9 o'clock a.m. a party reconnoitering accompanied the Commander in Chief and his staff . . . about 4 miles out and . . . after about two hours . . . returned . . . a little before sunset sent reconnoitering parties round the villages . . . but they returned without seeing anything to create the least suspicion, myself being one of the party. . . . We saw nothing about and in the afternoon sat down to make a dinner . . . thanks to one of the tent's crew who went out shooting yesterday, the fruits of whose labour was a fat buck, the haunch of which we had roasted together with some very savoury cutlets, this with the ever seasonable dish in India, currie and a little pastry completed the Christmas Dinner so that we had no reason to complain.'

His stomach had to take second place, as he described: 'but I had scarce seated myself to take a hearty meal and got a fine cutlet on my plate when ordered with two others to mount and accompany one of the Subaltern officers of the picquet, much to my annoyance. However, there was no alternative but to mount and away we went . . . on my return the picquet was mounted and had to sit there till after sunset. This is common practice throughout the British Army for all outposts to stand to their arms an hour at sunrise and also at sunset, during which time reconnoitring parties are sent out previous to extra sentinels being placed at night and withdrawn in the morning. When done the men then dismount and stand to their horses all night or lie at their heads in a state of vigilance.'

On Boxing day Godward noted: '26th December: Mounted our horses at daybreak at which time we were relieved. Arrived in camp completely fatigued and knocked up after the hard four and twenty hours' duty of yesterday . . . in this way was Christmas Day spent. . . . I hope the time is not far distant when I shall be able to partake of some Christmas festivals at home. . . . I don't know the day I was so completely knocked up as I was this morning for a more fatiguing picquet I never remember having done, for out of the 24 hours 18 of them I think were spent in the saddle. However, dispatching the morning dram soon got the tents pitched and the breakfast soon after appearing which was very speedily dispatched with an excellent relish, when to make up for yesterday indulged in an hour's refreshing sleep when again got merrily to work . . . as we are in expectations that an order will be issued for an advance.'

That evening he did a little belated celebrating, noting: 'Had an invitation from one of my old comrades to partake of a friendly glass of punch . . . spent a very convivial evening with a few select friends, pledged all dear friends and drank success to our arms in a bumper, sang a few songs after which the party broke up at about 10 p.m. at which time I set down to make up my journal. Contrary to my expectations no order to move. I believe the delay is to allow Major General Grey's division . . . to get one day nearer . . . to cut off the retreat of the fortress.'

The next two days they kept a series of picquets on duty all round but did not move and from Godward's journal it is clear that the camp was rife with rumour and counter-rumour. To begin with the enemy were within eight miles and preparing for an attack. Then it was said two of their generals had deserted and that General Grey was forced to detour a further forty miles to avoid a fortified pass. There was also the mixture of drama and farce common in warfare. On 28 December Godward recorded:

'The strictest vigilance in camp the whole of the night, but no enemy appeared. . . . News from the other division of the army who have made good their march . . . a party of Irregular Horse . . . was sent reconnoitering first thing this morning . . . led on by the brave Major General, who took them so close to the enemy's line as to be within range of shot . . . but . . . the only casualty . . . was a little Blenheim Spaniel belonging to Major General Churchill . . . they beat a retreat back to camp. . . . The orders for tomorrow are issued . . . the advance is made in three columns and by separate roads . . . the right column is composed as follows: Her Mjs 16th Lancers, 2 Troops of Horse Artillery, the Governor General's Body Guards 1st and 10th Native Cavalry. . . . The strictest watch to be kept in camp during the night and every man to be fully accoutred.'

The day of battle dawned and Godward in a rather hectic piece of writing mirrored the feelings of tension which most soldiers know at the prospect of imminent action. He wrote:

'29th December: Now comes the tug of war. With what light hearts and merry faces did every man arise from his hard pallet on this eventful morning and I never remember seeing the work done so speedily before. Every man stuck so willingly to it that the tents were struck and the camels loaded in half the usual time. . . . I don't know of any people who carry such an independent head as those who have the honour of calling themselves Her Mjs Dragoons . . . see them when you will they are the same.

'After waiting some time the trumpet sounded to horse. Our route this morning lay on the Bombay road which is the direct road to Gwalior. Every man appeared to me in the best of spirits puffing away cigars wholesale and relating tales and anecdotes much to the gratification of many . . . and . . . marched merrily along the road and at the end of the first two miles halted to allow the rear to close up, which done we went on again till we came to three cross roads and unable to judge the right one as we now turn off that we commenced our march on, but on the Major General referring to the plan of the Country which several officers with us were provided with, soon found the right one.'

After this first hiatus, when they obviously nearly took the wrong route, Godward was one of a small party selected by Major General Churchill and chronicled events as follows:

'A short distance from where these roads branch off stands a good sized village called Amoodghur. Round this the Major General and Governor General went reconnoitering with myself and 4 others out of my troop. On galloping up found there was an old fort and to our great astonishment found it contained a great number of Gwalior Infantry, who on our near approach showed themselves on the ramparts and bastions each armed with firelocks and bayonet, which pieces they were very deliberately loading. "Take care," says Major General Churchill. "And keep under cover of the wall (which was about forty yards from the fort) for these fellows mean mischief." However, [he] called a couple of villagers [over] who were at a short distance, who informed us that they were sent from the enemy's camp to procure grain. . . . "Very well," says the Major General. "We will have these fellows out." With such a small party as ours I fancy [this] would have been rather an hazardous undertaking had he still persisted in it. But the Deputy Major seeing the danger attending us interfering with so small a party as ours persuaded him against it.'

The fire-eating old general was still not satisfied and Godward continued: 'the brave old soldier boldly led the van . . . up to the fort walls and held a short conversation with them. They told the same story as the two villagers . . . but such a lot of careless, saucy fellows I never remember seeing. . . . After a short discourse we again continued round the village, at the back of which was much surprised to find a regular built barrack or row of huts the same as our own sepoy lines . . . capable of holding two or three hundred men, and seated outside several huts was a number smoking the hookah in a state of indolence.'

After this he was greatly relieved to rejoin his troop: 'Seeing nothing further to attract the attention we once more joined the column which had advanced some distance and I was not at all sorry to get so safe away from these rather formidable looking fellows, for had they thought proper to attack us we could not have made much resistance, although each of us exclusive of sword and lance had a carbine, which we took particular care to load on seeing these fellows do so. After a gallop of a mile over ploughed fields once more joined my troop and scarcely proceeded a mile further when we heard the enemy's guns opening fire on the other two columns.'

Then came the general action in which the 16th Lancers took their part:

'It was now about a ¼ to 8. Shortly after an aide de camp came galloping up with the intelligence that . . . Major General Thackwell was to move his division with as little delay as possible . . . on the aide de camp giving his orders we were formed in close column of squadrons and off we went at a pace the lazy Life Guards at home never dreamt of, the Artillery following close in our rear and in ten minutes came in sight of the enemy's line . . . and instantly into action where the busy scenes passing around chased away my thoughts of home. . . . On one column getting into action the two troops of Horse Artillery boldly dashed up in front of Maharajpore.'

During the night the enemy had captured the town and fortified it with cannon and picked infantry. Godward duly noted:

'This alteration in their position completely frustrated our mode of attack laid down this morning; however, our Artillery set to work in good earnest . . . dismounted a number of their guns . . . and silenced many. . . . The Infantry pushed into the town and carried it with the point of the bayonet . . . in less than an hour the whole town was in flames. The town blazed till long after sunset and . . . all that is left . . . is a mass of black ruins.'

While this attack was in progress the cavalry were ordered to turn the enemy's flank: 'We . . . had scarce proceeded a ¼ of a mile when we got it hot and strong on the right flank there being a field of standing corn which completely concealed a battery of 17 guns. It opened upon us a most murderous fire. In a very few minutes we lost upwards of twenty horses, three men killed and several wounded. Fortunately for us the guns were laid for infantry or our loss would have been considerable. Not a moment was to be lost. "Deploy into line," shouted our brave old General. "And charge the battery". It was done in an instant ... but great was our disappointment on arriving within half a pistol shot to find they were fronted by a deep ditch or ravine, which it was impossible to get cavalry over ... we paused but a few moments and retreated under raking fire. ... We were next ordered to protect our Artillery who were threatened by a large body of Mahratta Horse who on our near approach wheeled about and we saw no more of them.'

At this stage 'brave old General' Churchill was mortally wounded and carried off the field by a party of Lancers. Godward continued: 'We now charged a battery to the front, but with no more effect than the first time, for here again we found the same obstacle in a deep ditch and a deal of broken ground ... which showed good judgement on their part. ... Again we had to retreat and by some excellent manoeuvering drew their attention completely ... while the Infantry pushed up the ditch and carried the battery with ... the bayonet, killing every man who served it ...'

On 30 December Godward suffered what can only be described as a self-inflicted wound. He described events thus:

'No orders being issued for marching it was expected we should halt on this ground. ... On going out of the tent to wash ... I saw a large quantity of powder lying outside the tent. Thinking that some accident might occur I thought I would blow it up. ... I threw a piece of fire in amongst it and it was in I have no doubt for 2 minutes. ... I then stooped down ... [and] as soon as I touched the powder the whole exploded burning me very much up the right arm, face and nearly all the hair off my head. ... I went to hospital and was carried the day's march by four black fellows and for the first time for some years had a good cry, not with pain but with vexation for it was fully expected the enemy was not far in front of us and me stuck in hospital just at that critical moment. ... But as soon as we reached the next camp ground I spoke to the doctor. He gave me liberty to join my troop and believe me I did my duty for about a fortnight in real misery for at this time the duty was very hard. I was obliged to have the sleeve of my jacket open.'

The next day, the 31st, they remained halted and he commented:

'which we all stand much in need of as many things are out of repair and lost and want replacing . . . besides our horses are very much fatigued from their very severe work of late and stand much in need of rest. Quite contrary to our expectations this morning an order came to turn out in Review Order (which was no joke for me with my burnt face under the rays of a midday sun) for the reception of the young King and Queen of Gwalior who came to negotiate affairs with His Excellency and the Governor General. After sitting an hour these two noble personages made their appearance . . . His Majesty is a boy of 9 years. . . . His elephant was rather gaudily attired as was also the remainder in the train following . . . the whole passed up the street formed by our troops. They were received with a general salute as they passed along to the Durbar tents, where they remained . . . for about two hours.'

Godward and his 'comrade' seized the opportunity and got into conversation with a couple of the Rajah's followers:

'From their conversation I feel confident they were present at the action of the 29th . . . they said . . . the defeated troops . . . intend to show another front to us . . . but as these two men justly remarked, I think they may as well surrender without further bloodshed. . . . We then questioned these two fellows about the engagement of the 29th . . . and their hopes of victory were most sanguine until the town of Maharajpore was in flames and the cavalry had deserted them. . . . I then asked what they thought of British troops. . . . [He said] the Cavalry were noble men particularly the Lancers. The determined manner in which they made their advance galloping nearly to the mouth of the guns was beyond everything.'

The Durbar over, their officers put a stop to this fraternization. He noted: 'All officers present attended the Durbar and from their conversation it appears the young King sat and cried the whole time. . . . The interview lasted about 3 hours during which time we were seated on our horses exposed to the midday sun, which for the time of year is very hot and many men of weak constitution were taken to the rear fainting from the effects of it.'

New Year's Day, 1844, found him gloomy: 'How many dear friends who a twelve months ago were in the enjoyment of good health are now no more . . . and how buoyant was our hopes this time last year. Then I am sure I had not the remotest idea of being in India now, but fondly anticipating . . . favourable winds to dear old England. . . . A Salute was fired this morning in commemoration of the New Year. Nothing to do but Stable Parade. . . . Orders to march at 7 in the morning.'

On 2 January he recorded: 'Marched according to yesterday's orders. Had the pleasure of being on the hospital guard with the baggage. Having 46 camels under our charge had to fight my way through the greater part of the baggage and after much difficulty and many hearty curses from one and the other all of which we turned a deaf ear to and at last got clean down the road. . . . The army continued its march about 2 miles further and pitched their camp. . . . It is impossible to go any further in consequence of the immense quantity of baggage. On arriving in camp found to my discomfort that my squadron had gone on outlying picquet about a mile in advance. . . . The strictest watch ordered to be kept all day as a number of the Maharattas was round the villages here this morning.'

They had barely unloaded the baggage camels when he had to join a corporal and file of men to go with the Captain of the picquet, whose orders as quoted by Godward sound confusing:

'Trotted out a short distance and saw two or three dense clouds of dust as if arising from a large body of Cavalry. "Dismount Tubb and hold my horse," says the Captain, "till I see what this is . . . from the top of this mound." Made them out to be through the aid of a telescope a body of horse coming towards us. "These fellows mean something," says our gallant Captain. "Go back one man and tell the picquet to mount immediately and join us." . . . Up came the squadron. "Now men I have every reason to think these fellows mean to show us some sport. If they do, don't spare them an inch. Go into them and lick them, which I feel confident you can, was their numbers treble ours. Don't stand humbugging. Cut your way through them manfully and show them what European Lancers are. I don't want to have one of you hurt if possible and I know I can trust to every man never fear, but I will lead you into them. So be collected and if we find their numbers too much for us, which I don't think they are and have to retreat, keep well together. . . ." And off we went at a good round pace, but had scarce gone a mile towards them, every man full to the brim with the idea of being engaged on this important duty and the sensation the victory would cause in the camp . . . when the enemy perceived our advance . . . and cut away to the right as hard as if we were close on their heels much to our disappointment. . . . Their numbers I should judge to be about thrice ours which plainly show they are a mean and cowardly set of fellows.'

They then returned to their picquet, when he aired what sounds a very justifiable grievance: 'pitched our tents and sat down to a substantial breakfast, fully accoutred, which under existing circumstances can't say we enjoyed although our appetites were pretty keen after our morning's exertion. . . . I don't know of anything truly as miserable as sitting down to a meal with a stock on, which leather collars under no circumstances are allowed to be pulled off during the four and twenty hours duty. Oh what a treat and luxury it would be at times after a long gallop reconnoitering or patrolling to be allowed to pull off this infernal stock and have a souse in some good cold water, but (we are) compelled to dispense with water during these tours of duty excepting for drinking, which makes a man more weary than he otherwise would be. . . . Order to strike tents and pack baggage as soon as we dismounted, after which to lie at our horse's heads the whole of the night and in no circumstances is a man to unstrap his cloak.'

They had little or no rest: 'A constant patrol was kept up all night of 1 Sergt 1 Cpl and 8 privates who were patrolling . . . full two miles in advance . . . keeping us well up to it all night . . . at twelve o'clock we mounted . . . returning about two hundred yards to the rear. Here we dismounted and stood to our horses till after . . . the hour of 4 at which time we resumed our former position. The motive for this movement was, it being probable the enemy might pay the outposts a visit . . . how great would have been their surprise to find Cavalry in ambush for them, but as it was they thought better of it.'

The night's duty finally ended, he wrote: 'Was highly delighted to find . . . the cooks had prepared a fine kettle of coffee which proved truly acceptable this cold morning. Marched at 6 o'clock to the British residency of Gwalior . . . dismounted and stood to our horses a full 2 hours while the Quarter Master General marked out the camp ground, during which time I being so fatigued fell just at my horse's head with my lance cap for a pillow as did the two men with me, we being the leading files of the column and after an hour's sound sleep was awoke by my horse putting his nose in my face, at which I jumped up and frightened myself and horse, woke my two comrades and startled their horses and received a curse for so doing. . . . Did not get the camp settled until 4 o'clock. . . . I spent the whole of this day in bed having arrived in this ground completely fatigued and knocked up with the last twenty-four hours duty which was no joke (and doubly so to me for my arm was completely raw from the blowing up that I got on the 30th Dec). I don't know what some of the feather bed soldiers at home would think of it. In fact I much doubt if some would survive the duties done on this campaign.'

The 4th, 5th, 6th and 7th December were all spent at Gwalior, in a constant state of readiness, but thereafter the government agreed terms with the Maharajah, which included embodying the 10,000-strong army of the Mahrattas in a contingent force officered by officers of the Bengal army.

Godward continued his journal: 'On the 14th Inst. the Maharajah paid a visit to the Governor General and on his return I waylaid the procession . . . and took up my stand on a small hill by the road side, which was one complete street for 2 miles of Mahratta horsemen . . . and was rather surprised at the civil behaviour of these soldiers, who instead of insulting a single European unarmed amongst them gave me a Salaam and entered civilly and freely into conversation with me besides which made way for and gave me the most convenient place for seeing the procession pass and allowed me to examine their Arms most readily. I must pay them the just tribute of praise, which I think due to them . . . in my opinion they are the bravest and least treacherous of the Indian Nations. . . . They fought like brave and good soldiers, after the Battle behaved like men and I do not think one single instance has occurred of the cowardly midnight murders which happened so frequently in Afghanistan.'

He described the procession in some detail: 'the great Magnificent Maharajah . . . who poor little fellow followed all this route seated in a magnificent Howdah on an immense Elephant . . . and he kept his little hand continually touching his embroidered turban in acknowledgement of the many salaams and acclamations that he received. Poor child I doubt if he is as happy as I am. He has a troubled life in front of him, perhaps to be finished by a bloody end.'

The outposts had strict instructions that no European troops were to be allowed in the town of Gwalior in case of trouble with the Mahratta soldiers. Godward wrote: 'In spite of all this myself and comrade planned this walk and . . . passed the outpost Videts by going 2 miles round and after a good two hours walk came to the Mahrattas Camp . . . and was much surprised to see the very indolent way which the soldiers were going about . . . anything by way of duty was out of the question . . . some basking in the sun, others smoking the Hooka . . . these Mahrattas are very much addicted to drink and every other vice . . . and the many scenes of debauchery . . . surprised me . . . intoxication was to be seen in all its stages . . . being rather fatigued after our long ramble . . . we went up to one of these retailers of liquor . . . ordered a brass vessel full holding above half a pint and was much surprised to find he only demanded one Anna for it. Lit a cigar of a very mild flavour and stood gazing on the varied scenes around and not one of these drunken revellers interfered with us. . . . I was very sorry after reaching this far to be unable to visit the city, but time being pressing and besides the danger attending meeting officers prevented us from going and a breach of military discipline like this would be treated with the severest punishment.'

He and his comrade, however, did not go back by the long route they had taken and he wrote:

'We . . . passed through the outlying picquet much to the mortification of the Native Officer in Charge, at whom we enjoyed a hearty laugh, and persuaded him we had passed close to his post, but of course had to treat the old gent with civility although black. Reached camp tired enough and had the extreme mortification of getting ready for inlying picquet.'

On the 22nd the army was reviewed by the Commander in Chief and the Governor General and orders were given to disperse and march to cantonments, but unexpectedly on the 25th permission was given to visit the city and he and his 'comrade' duly took the opportunity 'after dispatching an early breakfast' to visit the town and especially the fortress on its massive rock. They were most impressed with the fortifications and the view. He wrote: 'On reaching the top . . . you find yourself surrounded by the building of the old palace and Zenanah. The latter presenting the most promising appearance we determined to explore it.'

They had difficulty finding the entrance and thereafter were nearly lost in a maze of rooms and passageways: 'sometimes . . . groping our way in the dark through places like dungeons. . . . So that we might be able to retrace our steps we marked the floor at every turning where we could get the least light. Fortunately I picked up a piece of chalk in one of the workshops with which Englishman like I had been scribbling my name on the walls of the rooms. For nearly two hours we thus rambled about.'

They finished their day's 'ramble' tired but pleased with themselves and the next day marched in pouring rain back towards Agra. He thereafter included a very lengthy description of the Taj Mahal, which he finally succeeded in visiting on his return march to Meerut. After his excursion round the Taj Mahal and Agra on 2 February he wrote: 'a few companions and myself adjourned to a toddy shop . . . to procure a bottle of Brandy, which having quaffed and pledged absent friends and from thence walked home delighted with our day's excursion and rather fatigued. We march tomorrow en route to Meerut but as we march by ourselves I shall here stop my journal.' Thus we are left with him enjoying a drink with his 'comrades' after a successful campaign.

The 16th Lancers remained in India until 1846 when they were in action again. As he wrote to his uncle on the 1st of February 1846: 'Our Regiment charged and broke up two Infantry Squares and captured several guns. The more I think of the affair the more it surprises me to think how we escaped. . . . I hope sincerely that in the next engagement I may come out as safe as this, without a scratch.'

He did survive the next engagement and returned with his regiment to England later that year. He was finally discharged in 1855 with a pension of £7 per annum as unfit for further service. Although always suffering poor health thereafter, he survived by reverting to his old trade as a barber and wigmaker in his native village until his death aged 52 in 1871, a belated victim of India's climate and diseases. His funeral was well attended by the local dignitaries and this ex-Lancer who had distinguished himself at the now-forgotten battles of Mahrajpoor, Ruddawal, Aliwal and Sobraon was buried with a degree of ceremony not previously accorded to him, thus proving that there's no hero like a dead hero.

CHAPTER SIX

Corporal George Coppard
1898–1984
Machine Gun Corps: 1914–1918:

'Every square yard seemed to be layered with corpses at varying
depths, producing a sickening stench . . . and once a head appeared
which wasn't there an hour before.'

George Coppard begins: 'I was just an ordinary boy of elementary school
education and slender prospects. Rumours of war broke out . . . and . . . I
knew I had to enlist. . . . Towards the end of August I presented myself to
the recruiting sergeant at Mitcham Road Barracks, Croydon . . . The
sergeant asked me my age and when told, replied: "Clear off, son. Come

back tomorrow and see if you're nineteen eh?" So I turned up the next day and gave my age as nineteen. . . . The sergeant winked as he gave me the King's shilling, plus one shilling and ninepence ration money for that day. I believe he also got a shilling for each . . . recruit . . . I enlisted on 27th August 1914. . . . I was sixteen years and seven months old. The Battle of Mons had just been fought and what was left of the Old Contemptibles was now engaged in the famous retreat. I knew nothing about all this.'

His first day was clearly imprinted on his mind: 'Our motley crowd of recruits shuffled up to East Croydon Station and took a train to Guildford, final destination Stoughton Barracks . . . headquarters of the West Surrey Regiment . . . The Queen's 2nd of Foot. . . . The regimental symbol was a lamb.'

He continued grimly: 'Reveille was at 5.30 a.m. next morning and after a night on the floor with half a blanket I didn't feel too good. Word flashed round that "gunfire" (tea) was available at the cookhouse. A scramble followed, but there were few mugs to drink from. I drank mine from a soup plate, not an easy task at first attempt. After a day or two of this sort of thing I realised . . . one had to hog it, or else run the risk of not getting anything at all. I learnt this lesson quicker than anything else.'

Their first task was pitching bell tents, in which they slept, the maximum 22 to a tent and, being the youngest, the wretched George Coppard drew the flap division. He recorded: 'Outside the tent flap within a yard of my head stood a urinal tub and throughout the night boozy types would stagger and lunge towards the tent flap to urinate. I got showered every time. . . . Luckily more tents became available and from then on I managed to avoid the entry flap.'

He noted: 'We were part of the new army being formed throughout the country, Kitchener's Army.' An interesting feature of the officer's uniform at this time 'was the stiff white collar worn with their khaki uniform. Junior officers wore khaki collars, but later on senior officers followed suit in favour of khaki neckwear. Maybe laundering difficulties had something to do with it.'

In November they moved to Sandling in Kent with thick snow on the ground. He noted: 'Life in the huts was miserable, especially as we were plagued with kit inspections every week. Our kit had to be laid out to a proper pattern and order; knife, fork, spoon, razor, comb, lather brush and so on. A good deal of pinching was going on and I found myself minus some articles. Deductions from pay for losses made me realize more than ever that I was in the army. The swiping of kit was a regular feature of life at Sandling and the only thing I could do was a bit of counter-swiping.'

Owing to the bad weather they moved to billets in Hythe, but their training continued and they marched from Hythe to Aldershot in February, 1915. He noted: 'Night operations, mock battles with blank cartridges, route marches in all weathers – all played their part in putting the finishing touches to our fighting fitness. . . . Two Vickers machine guns were now allotted to the battalion. Reserve teams were required and I was picked . . . and I became a keen and willing learner. The Vickers .303 water-cooled gun was a wonderful weapon . . . Devotion to the gun became the most important thing in my life for the rest of my army career.'

He recorded; 'Rumours of our impending departure for overseas began to spread. A hair-shearing parade was ordered and every N.C.O. and man had his hair shorn off close . . . The next thing to astonish us was an order abolishing the cleaning of buttons and other bright parts of our equipment. Every piece of brass had to be dulled like gun metal.'

They finally departed: 'Came 31st May 1915 and the battalion went on the binge, as it was our last night in Aldershot. The next day we left for Folkestone. A packet boat called the *Invicta* sneaked out of the harbour at 9.45 p.m. with the battalion on board, destination Boulogne.'

After a night in transit camp they had their first experience of train journeys in France: 'At the station the train, composed of covered freight trucks each marked 40 Hommes 8 Chevaux, lay waiting. After we had been told off in batches of 40 men there was a wild scramble to get on board, not an easy job with nearly three-quarters of a hundredweight of kit per man and forty rifles poking about. I sat on the side of the open doorway, legs dangling over the edge. The countryside looked beautiful and I felt as if I was taking part in a Sunday-school treat.'

They were clearly nothing like as fit as they should have been despite their months of training for after a short stop at St Omer they marched to Hazebrouck: 'a distance of 24 kilometres. Quite a number of men succumbed to the sun's heat . . . The fall-out rule of ten minutes each hour of marching was maintained, but after three or four hours fall-out became more like a collapse. Men literally crashed down with a great clatter of equipment and falling rifles . . . Junior officers had things a little easier for they marched in "light order", or with a dummy pack with little or nothing in it and a cane under the arm . . . the colonel and company c.o's, looking soldierly and unfatigued, rode well-groomed horses.'

They reached Meteren on the Belgian border. 'We had a pay parade while in the town: 5 francs per man. A franc was worth tenpence then, and ordinary wine cost half a franc a litre . . . We usually shared a litre of vin blanc which was more than enough to make us squiffy. Some of the houses displayed notices: "Oeufs et pommes de terre frites. 50 centimes". With a huge slice of country bread, plus a nip of cognac in the coffee the total cost was one franc and we felt grown up.'

On their final evening in Meteren they were formed into a square and told by the Colonel they were going into the trenches the following day. He warned them that any dereliction of duty such as 'desertion, mutiny, leaving the trenches without permission, cowardice and sleeping on sentry duty . . . would carry the death sentence. The C O then directed the adjutant to read out the names of nearly a score of Tommies who had recently been sentenced to death. . . . I was stupified as the adjutant droned out each man's name, rank, unit and offence. . . . The hour and the date of execution were also read out.'

Following this sombre introduction, the next day the battalion entered the trenches for the first time at Le Touquet near Armentières. He noted prosaically: 'Like everything else in life I soon found there was a routine to be followed in trench warfare. If the routine was upset by the outbreak of fighting it was resumed when the fighting ceased. I learnt that the front-line soldier was only concerned with the hundred yards or so on either side of him. His prime interest was to know all about that piece of land stretching between his part of the trenches and the German trenches in front of him, No Man's Land. He should know the exact distance across . . . any weaknesses in the barbed wire defences and the position of any ground features such as ditches, buildings and shell craters. Careful scrutiny by day, usually with the aid of a periscope, should provide him with a complete mental picture for use in the night hours.'

His description of the 'morning hate' is graphic: 'The day really began at stand-to. . . . The danger period for attack was at dawn and dusk. . . . About half an hour before dawn and dusk the order "Stand-to" was given and silently passed throughout the length of the battalion front. . . . Sentries stood on raised fire-steps peering over the parapet . . . towards Jerry's lines. The rest of the lads quietly relaxed. . . . Suddenly a German machine-gun, pre-set before darkness to fire on our parapet lets rip a devilish traverse. . . . Dirt is flung into faces and foul language seethes through everyone's lips. . . . Although there is no special cause for alarm intermittent rifle fire develops. . . . Jerry responds likewise for it is the morning hate.'

He noted: 'The military situation at Le Touquet was curious, for it seemed as if both sides . . . had tacitly agreed that this part of the line should be labelled "Quiet", it being understood that if one side started up any bloody nonsense the other side would follow suit. And that's how it was for days on end, except for snipers.'

This was a permanent danger. He wrote: 'Always there was the sniper, the loneliest and deadliest combatant in trench warfare, lurking like a jackal ready to strike. . . . There were latrines at intervals along the line, which generally took the form of small culs-de-sac cut in the back of the trench. The sites were shifted when necessary as Jerry snipers watched them very closely for the careless. Many a poor Tommy met his end in a latrine sap.'

The snipers were one of the major hazards at Le Touquet, as he made plain: 'Lulled by the quietness someone would be foolish and carelessly linger with his head above the top of the parapet. . . . A Jerry sniper with a telescopic-sighted rifle, nicely positioned behind the aperture of an armoured plate, has lain patiently for hours perhaps waiting for the slightest movement. . . . A pal of mine named Bill Bailey . . . died in this way.'

This was an incident which plainly made a great impression on him and he wrote: 'There were four of us in a short section of trench. It was early morning and stand-to was over. The fire was going nicely and the bacon was sizzling . . . just as I was about to tuck in Bill crashed to the ground. I'll never forget the sound of that shot as it found its billet. . . . A moment before Bill had been talking to us and now there he was breathing slightly, but otherwise motionless. I rushed round the traverse and yelled: "Pass the word along for stretcher-bearers!" We waited for them to come and for decency's sake put some bandages round Bill's head to hide the mess. Marshall and I volunteered to carry him to the first aid post. . . . On getting back to the front line we were both ravenous with hunger. My bacon and bread was on the fire-step but covered with dirt and pieces of Bill's brain. I looked down the front of my tunic and trousers and there were more bits there; my boots were sticky with blood. I felt the passing of Bill acutely as it was the first time a pal had been struck down beside me. It was a shock to realise that death could come from nowhere without actual fighting.'

He recorded the daily routine as follows: 'When daylight came the order "Stand down" passed along the line. Tension slackened but sentries still kept watch by periscope. . . . It was time for breakfast and each section made its own little fire. Charcoal was the official fuel but supplies were few and far between. Plundering for wood was a regular chore, but we never failed to produce a fire, slivering the wood with bayonets . . . to reduce the smoke. Soon the pungent whiff of bacon wafted round and life seemed good when billycans were filled with a fresh brew of tea . . . Weapon cleaning and inspection, always a prime task, would be followed by pick and shovel work. Trench maintenance was a constant job without an end. . . . The carrying of rations and supplies from the rear went on intermittently.'

The trenches at Le Touquet were in very good condition as he later discovered and their first sixteen days in the line ended on 6 July when the battalion was relieved. His conclusion was: 'Our Le Touquet spell taught us the value of strong and well-maintained trenches, with special attention being paid to parapets.'

It did not take them long to get accustomed to shellfire and Coppard wrote: 'The sound of four deep booms which seemed to come from well behind the enemy lines was my first indication of it. In a few moments I became aware of pulsating rushing sounds, increasing in power and intensity . . . and I knew instinctively the shells were heading in my general direction. The final vicious swipes of the projectiles as they rushed to earth turned my stomach over with fear which quickly vanished when four hefty explosions occurred in some ruined houses a hundred yards to the rear. This experience made me realise the value of a good pair of ears. Later on keen eyesight and practice enabled most of us in clear weather to pick out howitzer shells in the air, thus giving us a split second's grace to decide which way to dart for cover. The German 5.9 shells weighed about a hundred pounds and were generally referred to as 'coal boxes' . . . owing to the black smoke they gave off when bursting. Jerry artillery had an unpleasant habit of dispatching them in fours.'

He described an evening on sentry duty close to the front line in a deserted farmhouse: 'I stood in the avenue of trees . . . Brilliant flashes suddenly lit the sky behind the German lines and within a second or two came the sound of four consecutive booms from the howitzer battery. . . . Quickly the approaching coal-boxes tuned in midway between my ears and I knew I was in for trouble. There was a shallow trench beside me and as I flung myself into it the shells rushed to the ground, one of them striking a tree fifty feet away. The violence of the explosion . . . turned my inside over and deafened me. When I stood up it was difficult to control the trembling of my knees. Brutally aroused from slumber the platoon swarmed out of the barn.'

In August, unbelievably, he noted that 'the order was given to resume full spit and polish of equipment . . . it seems crazy, but that's how it was.' In September their spells of twelve days in the front line with breaks of four or five days in Armentières ended. On 29 September they were sent off as reinforcements to the Battle of Loos, which had already been going on for four days. As he noted: 'this was real war . . . There were over 60,000 British casualties and the battle lasted a month . . . with little or nothing to show for it.'

He described their approach march thus: 'Going up the communication trench at a snail's pace the battalion suffered casualties from shrapnel fire. As many troops were coming away from the front line as were going up. Stretcher bearers with the wounded, fatigue parties, telephone linesmen, runners and parties of relieved troops wended their way to the rear, jamming the narrow trench . . . Wrecked war gear lay about on both sides as we edged forward, including field guns, limbers and dead horses by the score. Blown up by internal gases their carcases were enormous and when punctured by shrapnel or bullets the foulest stench poisoned the air.'

At last they reached the site of the old German front line and here he described the horrific scene: 'Stretching for several hundred yards on the right . . . lay masses of British dead, struck down by machine gun and rifle fire. Shells from enemy field batteries had been pitching into the bodies flinging some about into dreadful postures. Being mostly of Highland regiments there was a fantastic display of colour from their kilts, glengarries and bonnets and also from the bloody wounds on their bare limbs. The warm weather had darkened their faces and shrouded as they were with the sickly odour of death it was repulsive to be near them. Hundreds of rifles lay about, some stuck in the ground by the bayonet, as though impaled at the moment of the soldier's death as he fell forward.'

Young Coppard was acting as a machine gunner for the first time and noted: 'On the way up to the front line I carried two boxes of machine gun ammunition, each containing 250 rounds in addition to my rifle and equipment. It was a heavy load, but the fact that I had been posted to the machine gun section kept me going for I was anxious to show that I could cope. . . .

'We gunners eventually took over a machine gun post in the Hohenzollern redoubt. I can't remember the name of the regiment whose gun team we relieved, but they were off like a shot as soon as our Vickers gun was mounted in place of theirs. . . . By then the Hohenzollern redoubt had developed a reputation as one of the worst spots in the whole of the trench system . . . The territory of the redoubt, a mass of pulverised dirt, covered no more than three or four acres, yet thousands fought and died there for months on end.'

He described this particular hell-hole with the eye of one who suffered it for a long time: 'The place consisted of a number of huge mine craters, roughly between the German front line and ours . . . so that there was in fact a more or less constant dispute for the possession of No Man's Land. Companies of Royal Engineers composed of specially selected British coal miners worked in shifts round the clock digging towards the German line. . . . A continual contest went on. . . . At the moment of explosion the ground trembled violently in a miniature earthquake. . . . Death or injury from the falling mass was a risk to friend and foe alike. There was nowhere to run for shelter in the crater area. Troops just pinned themselves to the side of the crater, muttered a prayer of some sort and cringed like animals about to be slaughtered.'

Coppard and his machine gun team had to spend eighteen days in this purgatory with the imminent possibility of being blown up by a mine as well as being shelled, sniped or machine gunned. He wrote later: 'Looking back I realise how fortunate I was that the Number One in my gun team was acting Lance-Corporal William Hankin, a brave cool customer from the forests of Hampshire. He was very fair with hair almost white and his cold grey eyes did more than anything else to help me control my fears. Nicknamed Snowy, he was a natural leader, and I treasure the memory of his friendship and courage.'

The Vickers gun was usually served by a six-man team. Number One, who fired the gun was the leader, and Number Two controlled the entry of the belts into the feed-block. Number Three maintained the supply of ammunition to Number Two and the remainder were carriers and reserves, all fully trained in each other's tasks. When fired at night a drainpipe cover was fitted over the muzzle to prevent the sparks being seen except from immediately in front, when the enemy would generally be too busy taking cover to mark the position accurately. Although used mainly in defence it was also used to provide covering fire in attacks.

It was at this stage that he recorded a new terror weapon: 'Following a dull thud from close behind the enemy lines, we saw our first "minnie", fired by a mortar gun Jerry called a Minnenwerfer (mine-thrower). The missile was made from a steel drum, packed with high explosive and scrap iron. When fired the thing sailed up in the air to a hundred feet or so with a lighted fuse trailing from it, describing a graceful curve as it travelled towards our lines. . . . There was a couple of seconds to decide which way to run. . . . The explosion was devastating and threatened to tear one apart by concussion. The devilish trail of a minnie curving towards him put fear in the heart of the bravest. Trenches were blasted into ruts. Incessant pick and shovel work was necessary to restore anything resembling a parapet. . . . Men just disappeared and no one saw them go. A weary Tommy would scratch a hole in the side of the bottom of a trench to get out of the way of trampling feet. A minnie would explode and the earth above him would quietly subside on him. . . . In one stroke he was dead and buried.'

For Coppard and his machine-gun team their first night must have been bad enough. He wrote: 'The combined roar of minnies and of bombs exploding in the craters went on incessantly. . . . We kept anxious watch . . . Once a Jerry machine gun not more than eighty yards away opened fire, giving off a vivid spout of sparks. Snowy promptly silenced it, firing half a belt straight at it . . . Before dawn stand-to was ordered, but we treated this as a poor sort of joke. Dawn came, and we looked a haggard lot as we munched bully and biscuits washed down with tepid water. Tea making was out. The surest way to invite disaster was to start a fire. . . .

'Crater fighters were considered to have a pretty mean chance of survival, twelve hours being reckoned as the limit a survivor could stand and keep his reason. Before starting a twelve hour shift in a crater each man had to complete a field postcard for his next of kin leaving the terse message "I am quite well" . . . many . . . [were] dead within the hour . . .'

After their first night on the edge of the crater area his team learned they were to have a spell in the craters themselves. 'So we filled in the field postcards . . . and with gun and gear crept into a flanking crater. There was barely room for the six of us on the lip. . . . At the bottom of the crater was a pile of corpses, some British, some German. I found it hard to keep my eyes away from them. No matter where I looked I could not avoid them. . . . It was an immense relief to get out of the crater at the end of our shift. We had been lucky. Because our position was on a flank any rifle grenades which had come our way had overshot to the back of the crater. In a sense being relieved was out of the frying pan into the fire, for we were back in the minnie area . . . The Germans seldom used minnies against our craters which were too close to their own. . . . In twelve hours another spell of crater duty awaited us.'

Coppard obviously knew from bitter experience what he was talking about when he wrote with a remarkable degree of understatement: 'Prolonged exposure to siege warfare conditions of the type which prevailed in the Hohenzollern redoubt seriously affected the morale and nervous systems of men not physically capable of endurance. If any poor devil's nerves got the better of him and he was found wandering behind the lines, a not infrequent occurrence . . . there was no psychiatric defence available to help save him from a firing squad. . . . It is my considered opinion that some men who met their end before a firing squad would have willingly fought the enemy in hand-to-hand combat, but they simply could not endure prolonged shell and mortar fire.'

Their rations appear to have been in very short supply when in this notorious redoubt. Water was in such short supply that shaving was not permitted, bread was seldom seen and loose rations 'such as tea, cheese and meat' were all 'tipped into a sandbag, a ghastly mixture resulting. In wet weather their condition was unbelievable and you could bet the rats would get at them first.' Coppard noted that he never received an apple or an orange as part of his rations.

The Battalion was relieved after nearly three weeks in action on 18 October, when they 'trudged back to Verquin, a village near Béthune. We were done up and severely shocked by our experiences. . . . A full day's rest allowed us to clean up a bit and to launch a full scale attack on lice. I sat in a quiet corner of a barn for two hours delousing myself as best I could. We were all at it for none of us escaped their vile attentions. The things lay in the seams of trousers, in the deep furrows of long thick woolly pants and seemed impregnable. . . . A lighted candle applied where they were thickest made them pop like Chinese crackers. After a session of this my face would be covered with small blood spots from extra big fellows . . . Lice hunting was known as "chatting". If a chap said he was going for a "chat" we knew what he meant.'

To a young seventeen-year-old, still a growing lad, food, of course, was tremendously important and he wrote: 'The battalion cooks got busy with the field-kitchens, and life began to glow in us with the sweet smell of bacon frying. A familiar cry I loved to hear was, "Roll up for your dip!" This was the hot swimming bacon fat in which one could dip a slice of bread. Experience told me to drop everything and run like hell to get in quick. Sometimes the cooks poured an extra tin of condensed milk into the big dixies of tea. The toffee-like brew seemed delicious to my young palate. Bully beef stew, too, tasted jolly good when one hadn't had a hot meal for three weeks.'

After only a week's respite behind the lines they returned to Vermelles and he acknowledged: 'The noise of bombing in the redoubt area renewed the sensation of fear in the pit of my stomach.' But they returned to the front line a little to the left of the ghastly redoubt area in front of a feature called 'Fosse 8', which was a large slag heap around eighty to a hundred feet high and over a hundred yards long. Coppard wrote: 'With the big Fosse looming directly in front of us we felt naked and wide open to enemy observation.'

In many ways their life was little better than in the notorious Hohenzollern redoubt.

'As we were on the fringe of the redoubt, the minnie threat extended to our area and many dead were churned up in bits and pieces. Every square yard seemed to be layered with corpses at varying depths, producing a sickening stench. We would curtain off protruding parts with a sandbag, pinned to the side of the trench with cartridges. A swollen right arm with a German eagle tattooed on it used to stick out and brush us as we squeezed by, and once a head appeared which wasn't there an hour before. When attempted concealment was useless, we'd chop off the putrid appendages and bury them. So long as we were alive we had to go on living, but it wasn't easy with the dead sandwiched so close to us. We took our meals and tried to sleep with them as our neighbours. Amid laughter and bawdy stories they were there.'

In such a sub-human atmosphere they had to have safety-valves and one of these, as Coppard rightly pointed out, was the use of constant foul language: 'It must be acknowledged that in most of the situations that Tommies had to contend with bad language was the only kind that made sense. The adjective derived from the four letter word held pride of place in our limited vocabulary. . . . A pent-up bloke felt good after delivering a particularly foul and original sentence and his face would beam at the cheers which acclaimed his efforts.'

Rats as well as lice made their life in the front line miserable: 'Rats . . . were a powerful contributory cause of some of the language used. They bred by the tens of thousands . . . When we were sleeping in funk holes the things ran over us, played about, copulated and fouled our scraps of food, their young squeaking incessantly. There was no proper system of waste disposal in trench life. Empty tins of all kinds were flung away over the top on both sides of the trench . . . During brief moments of quiet at night one could hear a continuous rattle of tins moving against each other. The rats were turning them over.'

They had a twelve-day session in Fosse Eight followed by six days in reserve. He noted at this point: 'Executions became a subject of much earnest conversation, especially when a list of names was published. Personally I was horrified at this terrible military law and I was scared stiff . . . I would be picked for a firing squad. . . . To be honest, I don't think I would have refused. The code of slavish obedience to orders given, no matter what, was as strong in me as in all volunteers then. That was the important thing about the volunteer system. . . . A man was challenged, not compelled, to fight for his country and all that it entailed. A volunteer seldom failed to meet the challenge because of an inborn pride at being a volunteer.'

Not surprisingly Coppard wrote: 'Our six days' rest passed like a flash. From . . . comparative seclusion . . . we were pitched into some kind of Dante's inferno again.' This was late November but they still had not been issued with any winter clothing to withstand the bitter nights. In his diary he merely recorded laconically: 'Heavy shelling and mortars here. Very cold.'

After another ten days in action they were relieved and this time after a short spell in reserve they marched 20 kilometres to a hamlet near Lillers well behind the lines. Understandably he recorded: 'Each step we took was in the right direction . . . as we marched our spirits soared in spite of our 8olb load.'

They rested in the back area for fourteen days during which the machine gun section had intensified training and was doubled in size to four Vickers guns. On 6 December they marched back to Béthune and spent a night in an empty tobacco factory before taking over a stretch of trench at Givenchy, five kilometres north west of the Hohenzollern redoubt.

'The trenches were full of liquid mud which reached up to our knees.

With the absence of proper dugouts and no dry place to sleep, we were soon in a wretched state. It rained cats and dogs and the nights were pitch dark and bitterly cold. On gun duty the hours dragged by with excruciating tedium and hunger. . . . I was ravenous. . . . [It] had all the elements of a most unpleasant spell; Prussian troops facing us across No-Man's Land, minnies and waterlogged trenches.'

Despite the vaunted belligerency of the Prussian troops the machine gun section to which Coppard was attached survived this sixteen-day spell in action with few casualties. Nevertheless it is easy to understand their pleasure at being relieved on the 18th. 'The battalion returned to Béthune and rested in the tobacco factory. It was sheer luxury to get a share of a dry clean floor to sleep on. The cooking arrangements were good too. "Burgoo" (porridge) before the breakfast fry-up and spotted dog (currant pudding) with dinner were welcome fillers.'

They only had four days rest before the battalion was sent to the trenches at Festubert on 23 December. Here he wrote, 'the front-line area was flooded and the communication trenches had vanished under water. There was no front-line trench. Instead earthworks, constructed of sandbags piled up on top of the original parapet, had been made. These earthworks . . . were like islands jutting out of the water about twenty yards long and spaced out every three of four hundred yards. A Vickers gun team was posted on each island to defend the line while the rest of the battalion kept in the rear clear of the swamp.'

Before being sent forward the machine gun sections were provided with thigh-length rubber boots, which were splendid in theory provided the water did not come over the tops. In the circumstances prevailing, however, it should have been foreseen that this was inevitable. In the event they were only approaching their 'island' when heavy machine gun fire forced them to crouch down and 'water poured into our boots and two poor devils fell over, completely immersed.' Looking back he wrote: 'I always think of my time there as one of the worst of my experiences, not so much because of the enemy action, but because of the miserable conditions. . . .

'The gun team we relieved spoke in whispers and told us they could hear the Germans talking. Wishing us a happy Christmas the relieved team crept away like ghosts and we were left in the inky blackness. It was in fact 23 December, 1915 and we were to be stuck on the island for four days. . . . When daylight came we realised there was barely four feet of cover . . . unable to stand we waited as the hours dragged on, longing for darkness so that we could stretch our limbs a little.'

On Christmas Eve they were visited by a 2nd Lieutenant: 'He came to remind us that . . . there was not to be any fraternising with the enemy on Christmas Day. The whole world knew that on Christmas Day 1914 there was some fraternising at one part of the line. . . . Speaking for my companions and myself . . . we were in no mood for any joviality with Jerry. In fact after what we had been through since Loos we hated his bloody guts. . . . [The 2nd Lieutenant] was shot through the head shortly after arriving on the island. A machine gun swept the breastwork and got him. He died . . . in the early hours of Christmas Day . . . another case of a life thrown away because a man was tall. . . . [He] was a giant. . . . It was bad enough for me at five feet nine and a half to remember the height of a parapet.'

Christmas Day, 1915, could scarcely have been worse for this small isolated unit: 'Our thoughts turned to home and our loved ones. . . . No letters came; no parcels; nothing. The soggy rations were of the meanest kind, the only pretence at Christmas being a few soggy raisins covered with hairs and other foreign matter from the inside of a sandbag. . . . Stretcher-bearers came after dark for the young officer.'

That night, however, they revenged his death, as they saw it, for they heard the sounds of activity in front and Coppard wrote:

'It was the most careless bit of enemy movement we had ever heard. . . . Snowy and I reckoned that it was a wiring party not more than eighty yards away. . . . Leaving the rest of the team we took the Vickers with muzzle-extension attached and a full belt of ammo. Stealthily working our way thigh deep in water we came to a point fifty yards clear of the island and lay on a mound of wet earth. . . . I fired a Verey light into the darkness and . . . revealed . . . twenty or more Jerries spread out by their wire. . . . Swiftly . . . Snowy plied the hail of bullets. . . . The ground where the enemy had fallen was raked across the width as they lay to finish off any crafty one who might be feigning death. . . . That was good enough for us. Wading back we joined our companions. . . . The age-old sentiment of "goodwill to all men" meant nothing to us then.'

They were relieved on the fifth night and Coppard wrote: 'Back we plodded to the welcome dry warmth of the Béthune tobacco factory. The ten-kilometre journey . . . was exhausting in thigh boots. Before I could flop down there were things to be done. I had to secure a little bit of floor space to lie on; scramble for blankets and rations; remove mud-encrusted clothing from the waist downwards revealing the half-pickled skin beneath; deal with any irritant lice; and keep an eye cocked in the direction of my possessions for fear of swiping – all these jobs and several others just had to be done. Then ... I could slip under the blankets into unconsciousness.'

They were only allowed four days rest before returning for a further nine-day spell in the front line, then a further four days' rest before yet another five days on the 'island'. Finally on 18 January the division was relieved for the first time since Loos at the end of September, after nearly three months in action. Coppard wrote: 'We marched out of the war area to Gionnheim, a drab village five kilometres from Béthune. . . . Number 13 Platoon was billeted in the cosy loft of a barn, full of luxurious hay and straw. Rats ran along the beams and rifled our packs, but we didn't worry. All we wanted was warmth and plenty to eat.'

It is clear that at this stage young Coppard was dangerously near to suffering battle fatigue. Then on 24 January he was ordered to report to the orderly room, where he learned that his stepfather, a sergeant serving with the East Surreys, had been killed. He was granted compassionate leave to visit his mother and noted: 'My outstanding regret was that a meeting which my stepfather and I had been trying to arrange could not take place.'

He arrived home on leave on 26 January, 1916, his 18th birthday. He recorded the memory with warmth: 'It had become the fashion to welcome home troops at Victoria Station. People pressed forward . . . and gave me packets of cigarettes and chocolate. Religious organisations provided lashings of buffet fare and hot drinks. It was just marvellous for a Tommy's homecoming. Leave men carried their rifles and this usually indicated that they had arrived from the front. Most people knew this and when I went into a pub at East Croydon it never cost me a penny. It was a wonderful thing to feel that people really did care. . . . The wrench came when I had to say goodbye and return to France. Heart-breaking scenes occurred when the troop trains departed. I was in tears. With the companionship of other Tommies . . . I soon forgot the tears.'

On 5 February the 37th Machine Gun Company of the Machine Gun Corps was formed and the section of the Queen's Own to which Coppard belonged was incorporated in it. There followed a period of intensive training to bring them up to fresh standards of efficiency in the new

Corps. Towards the end of February they were marched to Vermelles and straight into the line. His section was in support of the Queens in the Hohenzollern redoubt, the sensible idea being that as far as possible each section was posted to support its old regiment.

For a short period Coppard was given the job of batman to a Lieutenant Wilkie. He noted several differences in his new life:

'Instead of being stuck in the front line I shared with Mr Wilkie a half-completed German dugout in a support trench. It had twenty steps leading down to a fair sized room with hefty timber supports. There was only one entrance facing the wrong way. The location was well within minnie range and a hit on the entrance would have been disastrous . . . Compared with the lot of my pals . . . the dugout was a "little bit of heaven".'

Lieutenant Wilkie, a twenty-year-old Scot from Croydon, treated him as a comrade but also proved a conscientious officer visiting the four guns in his charge frequently, always accompanied by Coppard, who wrote: 'When on patrol my role was that of body-guard (and) guide . . . in the dugout, I looked after the grub side. . . . The rations were the same as for the men, but they looked better. We ate together, sang songs and indulged in a game of cribbage occasionally.'

Coppard noted the difference between the life of the officers and the men thus: 'Their greatest comfort was sleeping bags and blankets and room to stretch out for sleep. Batmen were handy to fetch and carry. Meals and drinks were prepared and placed before them. In addition to rum, whisky was available. . . . Cartoons and pin-ups decorated the walls and there was never a lack of the precious weed. Such things and many other small trifles demonstrated the great difference between the creature comforts of the officers and the complete absence of them for the men. That's what war was like.'

With a heavy fall of snow patrolling became difficult. After six days they had five days rest in Béthune before returning to the same sector where the fighting had become even more ferocious. In those fourteen days alone the casualties amounted to 3,000 men. Coppard recorded:

'On the night of the 18th of March the enemy shelled our lines heavily with gas shells and in the general confusion . . . attacked and captured A and C craters. . . . Gas helmets were worn for three hours and I was nearly suffocated. The helmet was nothing more than a flannel bag soaked in a chemical solution with a piece of mica for a window which soon steamed up . . . Gas was a devilish weapon against which these early masks made it impossible to measure one's chances of survival.'

The use of gas was not the only aspect of the all-out warfare being practised in this area. He continued:

'B Company of the Queens were victims of a villainous trick by the Prussians during this spell. Three hundred of them came across No Man's Land feigning surrender, with no rifles or equipment, their hands held high, but with pockets full of egg bombs. Just before reaching our wire they flung themselves to the ground and hurled a rain of bombs into B Company's trench causing many casualties . . . Most Vickers gunners swore a private vendetta. From then on the advance of a crowd of Jerries with their hands up would be the signal to open fire.'

On 19 March they were relieved and retired to Béthune. Ten days later they were back in the hellish Hohenzollern redoubt, but the bitterly cold weather had added to their miseries. They had been issued by this time with winter clothing consisting of sleeveless fur-lined leather jerkins and Balaclava hats with ear flaps and mittens, but as Coppard pointed out: 'it was almost impossible to achieve sufficient movement to circulate the blood properly. For men huddled in a few feet of trench, or in the craters it must have been murder. The officer and I were lucky in having to patrol the four guns covering over half a mile to do so, after which we sweated like bulls . . . Many cases of trench feet developed. This was a pickling of the skin and flesh caused by the persistent cold and wet and hospital treatment was a long business. Tins of whale oil were supplied for rubbing into the feet. I rigorously kept up this drill and my feet never bothered me.'

Lieutenant Wilkie fell sick with a feverish cold and Coppard accompanied him to hospital as his batman. When he had recovered Coppard himself fell sick. They were both back in action in the Hohenzollern redoubt for Easter, however, when two German mines blew up simultaneously, causing considerable British casualties. Finally they were relieved on 25 May and marched to the village of Allouagne near Lillers.

Here they spent time training and indulged in sports. It was here that Coppard saw 'two military policemen . . . with a handcuffed prisoner . . . in full view of the crowd and villagers, tied him to the wheel of a limber cruciform fashion. The poor devil, a British Tommy, was undergoing Field Punishment Number One and this public exposure was part of the punishment. There was a dramatic silence as every eye watched the man being fastened to the wheel . . . Lashing men to a wheel in public in a foreign country was one of the most disgraceful things in the war. Troops resented these exhibitions but they continued until 1917.'

On 27 June they marched for the Battle of the Somme, when 26 British and 14 French divisions lost approximately three quarters of a million casualties between 1 July and 20 November to capture a piece of land about seven miles square. By this time Coppard was back as Number Two on Snowy Hankin's gun team. They were now armed with .45 revolvers instead of rifles and equipped with steel hats for the first time.

On 1 July they were in action and eventually mounted their Vickers in the British advanced trenches from which the attack had started. He wrote: 'We brought in a number of wounded men who had fallen near our trench and bandaged them up. . . . With a British casualty figure of 60,000 on the first day of the struggle it was beyond the power of man to give aid except to a few.'

He continued: 'The next morning we gunners surveyed the dreadful scene in front of our trench. . . . Hundreds of dead, many of the 37th Brigade, were strung out like wreckage washed up to a high-water mark. Quite as many died on the enemy wire as on the ground, like fish caught in a net. They hung there in grotesque postures. Some looked as though they were praying; they had died on their knees and the wire had prevented their fall. . . . The Germans must have been reinforcing their wire for months. It was so dense that daylight could barely be seen through it.'

He went on to point out that the Generals should have known that artillery fire did not pound the wire to pieces, but merely lifted it up and dropped it down, often as a worse obstacle than before. As Coppard wrote grimly: 'Someone had blundered about the wire.'

Inevitably the machine-gun section had their near misses. On one occasion the gun itself was flung in the air when a coal-box landed between the legs of the tripod, but fortunately failed to explode. On another occasion three of the team were buried by another coal-box which exploded over the dugout in which they were sheltering.

While bandaging a casualty on one occasion Coppard realised his injuries had been caused by dum-dum bullets and he noted: 'Later on, we found several clips of German soft-nosed bullets and, as opportunity offered, experienced grim satisfaction in shooting them back with Mauser rifles. Such action was probably against international conventions, but we knew nothing about such things. We did know that Jerry was using saw-edged bayonets, flame-throwers and poison gas when it suited him.

Simple justice demanded that whatever he used against us was meet and proper for him to get back.'

They were relieved on 9 July: 'Exhausted, filthy and crawling with lice,' but they were back again on the 25th relieving the Australians near Ovillers and he noted: 'We mounted the Vickers in the old German front line of 1st July. Our dead were still hanging on the wire, but were shortly removed and buried. It was staggering to see the high standard of trenches that the Jerry front-line troops had used. We envied the skill and industry used in constructing such comfortable yet powerful defences. Some of the dug-outs were thirty feet deep with as many as sixteen bunk beds, as well as door bells, water tanks with taps and cupboards and mirrors.'

He pointed out once again where the High Command had been woefully lacking: 'the deep dugouts had withstood everything that our heavy artillery had thrown at them. . . . It certainly wasn't the fault of the British Tommy that he had to put up with scratch holes instead of decent dugouts. If he had been given the materials and proper instruction, not only would he have had a better life, but thousands of lives would have been saved.'

By this time he was Number One on his own team, but still remained friendly with his old Number One, Snowy Hankin. They enjoyed testing the British steel helmets lying around with a pick. He noted: 'A good British helmet yielded only a moderate dent, but a dud would burst open. . . . Clearly some cunning war contractor had been cheating and a War Office check had not been properly carried out.'

He also recorded: 'Collecting military badges from the dead was indulged in by many. I wore a broad leather belt that was covered with them. . . . Ghoulish curiosity drove me to turn over Jerry corpses for souvenirs and I got a couple of watches and a Luger pistol. One of the watches had a natty bell alarm . . . It came in useful for ringing the night hours to mark the changing of the gun reliefs.'

On 21 August they took over some machine gun posts near Rivière opposite Blairville on the edge of an orchard where there were some fruit trees still standing and bearing fruit. In the dark they used to pick the fruit in spite of periodic German machine gun fire through the trees until one day Coppard was caught up a tree as a flare was sent up and the orchard raked by machine gun fire. After that they stopped the practice and he wrote: 'We were all bloody idiots and dead lucky not to suffer casualties.'

On 28 September, after being relieved, they were sent aboard Paris buses to Albert. A new phase of the Somme battle had started and on the 1st of October they marched to Delville Wood, 'the scene of terrible fighting a few days earlier . . . The road banked on either side was full of British and German dead. In the darkness we kept stumbling over the bodies and when I fell heavily on one it gave out a deep grunt. The sudden weight of my body had compressed the corpse, forcing gases through the throat. . . . Somebody laughed, but I felt far from laughter as I struggled to get the tripod once more on my shoulder.'

He noted: 'Stand-to was on when we slithered into the shallow front-line trench . . . an attack appeared imminent. . . . I opened fire to discourage . . . any attack. . . . Without the Vickers Jerry would have walked into our trench as the infantry had suffered severe casualties. . . . Three days in that place exhausted us as we had very little sleep. . . . Two guns teams . . . relieved us on the fourth night, taking over our guns and ammo.'

On their way back he wrote: 'the enemy shrapnel was hellish' and at some point he dropped his revolver. He noted: 'Like a mug I went back. I soon found that being alone . . . was very different from being with my pals. . . . The further I stumbled . . . the more windy I became. There was some moonlight, and although it helped me pick my way, it more clearly showed the piles of dead. My worst fear was being killed without a pal knowing about it. A pal would recover my pay book and . . . write a letter of condolence to my next-of-kin. . . . Systematically I covered many square yards. . . . My hand touched a piece of cord . . . the lanyard, which . . . had broken. . . . On the way back I . . . got lost. . . . I had been away four hours.'

On 17 October he was wounded in the foot by his great friend Snowy Hankin, who accidentally pulled the trigger of his .45: 'The bullet tore between two bones in front of the ankle . . . and buried itself in the ground.' He was carried to a field dressing station and his friend was put under open arrest, pending an enquiry. Initially he found himself in a casualty clearing station as a suspected Self-Inflicted Wound case. The mistake was soon cleared up, fortunately for him as SIW casualties were given a tough time and little sympathy, as he discovered before the mistake was rectified. He was then soon on a hospital ship for home where he spent the next six months convalescing.

On returning to active service again he went through an unpleasant re-introduction to service life with a spell of parade ground drill at the hands of merciless instructors and was relieved to get back to France and report back at last to his old company on 8 May, 1917. His friend Snowy Hankin was now a corporal, but other old friends had died. He noted: 'I soon fell into the old routine. My sudden plunge into the fighting area again brought back that wind-up feeling under shell-fire and it was not easy to control. The daily comradeship of my pals . . . gave me strength. To most of us it was no longer a matter of patriotism any longer – that had burned itself out long ago. What remained was a silent bonding together of men who knew there was no other way out but to see the thing through. Deep down, too, was an implacable hatred of the Huns, for all the misery and death they had caused.'

On 18 June they marched towards Arras and the next day they were held in reserve helping with odd jobs: 'On several occasions I helped to repair the front-line wire, a nerve-wracking job. Dreading bursts of machine-gun fire we worked in silence at top pressure until dawn crept up. We made many trips carrying boxes of . . . ammo up to the front line, a journey of over two miles. . . . The last quarter of a mile under severe shell fire was cruel and I was drenched in sweat.'

He recorded the death of one of his team as follows: 'German shelling in the Wancourt area was the heaviest I had yet experienced . . . miraculously my team suffered no casualties . . . [then one] was killed outright. When the shelling lulled a bit, three of us took him to a patch near Foss Farm, and I'm afraid buried him in a great hurry, for the blasted Hun began dropping crumps almost on the place. "Goodbye old pal" were the only words said. Two crossed sticks were stuck in the mound and we hurried back to the front trench. . . . In a small unit like a machine gun team it was a deep and personal loss when a comrade was killed and the bond of friendship broken for ever.'

Through July and August 1917 the team was on varied duties from anti-aircraft work to trench support fire. Coppard wrote: 'For anti-aircraft work a circular pit was dug and the Vickers was mounted on a post in the centre. This allowed a full circle of fire. Enemy airmen were quick to notice a blind spot directly above the gun which would not operate at too steep an angle. A sharp lookout had to be kept. . . . Once a Boche plane sneaked up from behind and from 200 feet dropped a bomb which only missed us by a few feet. As he sped off on a straight course . . . I helped him on his way with a long burst which included tracers.'

He continued: 'From September to early November the company

continued in and out of the Monchy and Wancourt lines, with no promise of a break-through. . . . I was promoted Corporal in October . . . in November I contracted influenza, which put me in hospital for eight days.'

On the night of 19 November the division moved up to prepare for the Battle of Cambrai. Coppard recorded: 'Zero was at 6.30 am that memorable day, 20th November. We heard the sound of tank engines warming up. . . . A vast drum of terrible thunder swept along the eight mile front and a chorus of shells screamed to the east. . . . The tanks looking like giant toads became visible against the skyline as they approached the top of the slope . . . We went forward into enemy country in a manner never possible without the aid of tanks. . . . It was broad daylight as we crossed No Man's Land and the German front line. . . . I saw remarkably few Jerries about dead or alive.'

Coppard concluded that with fourteen months' warning the Germans had been ready for the assault when it finally came. He finally reached his objective and placed his two guns with two other guns on his left, of which he took command as senior NCO. Behind them was a German artillery dugout which they used as their HQ.

'Nightfall came and a German . . . battery . . . began shelling very near our positions. . . . [It] was in a vulnerable position . . . and it was well within our range. . . . As a protest and for the good of morale, two of the Vickers guns ripped off a belt each at the battery. The rain of fire had almost instant success, and we had no further trouble that night.'

On 22 November, 1917, he was severely wounded. His description was as follows: 'At 8 a.m. Lieutenant Garbutt, a lance corporal and myself were . . . discussing features of the local terrain . . . a hail of bullets clove the air. I fell as a bullet passed clean through the thickest part of my left thigh, severing the femoral artery. . . . When the gun stopped my two companions bravely got to work and when they ripped open the leg of my trousers a spout of blood curved upwards like a scarlet arc, three feet long and as thick as a pencil. . . . To stop the blood I bunged my thumb on the hole. . . . The lance corporal rigged up my bootlaces as a tourniquet and lashed it round my thigh above the wound. . . . A batch of Jerry prisoners came along under escort and the officer arranged for four of them to carry me to the first aid post.'

That was virtually the end of Coppard's war. He wrote: 'Within an hour or so I was in a field hospital under canvas. The surgeons did their job in a large marquee. When I came to I saw two half-inch rubber tubes extending through the bandages round my thigh. The travelling instructions called for Lysol to be squirted through the tubes every two hours. I was a blighty case without a doubt and in a few hours I was . . . bound for Southampton.'

Despite two failures of the ligatures resulting in haemorrhages in those days before blood transfusions were known, he slowly recovered. The news from the front by 2 December, however, was that all the gains from the Battle of Cambrai had already been lost through lack of sufficient reserves to consolidate the gains. News came through in January that Coppard himself had been awarded a well-deserved Military Medal. By the end of June, 1918, he was discharged from hospital and he joined the Machine Gun Corps convalescent home in Alnwick. He was then posted to Harrowby but still category B. He was there when the war ended and was demobbed shortly after his 21st birthday after four and a half years' service.

He wrote: 'My leg had shrunk a bit and I was given a pension of twenty five shillings per week for six months. Dropping to nine shillings per week for a year the pension ceased altogether. . . . As a Corporal I received about twenty eight pounds as a gratuity. . . . Demobbed men were allowed to keep their army overcoats, but . . . could hand them in at any railway station and receive one pound. . . . I traded mine in for a quid. It took all my gratuity to clothe me into something resembling a civilian.'

Without any civilian training Coppard, and thousands like him, felt severely handicapped after the war. He was unemployed for several months and, after an initial job as assistant steward in a golf club, he became a warehouse clerk in Greenock in Scotland. Then he became a waterguard officer with the Customs and Excise Department, transferring eventually to the Ministry of National Insurance and retiring in 1962. He died in 1984, aged 86.

CHAPTER SEVEN

Lieutenant Edwin Campion Vaughan
1898–1931
War Diary 1917: Passchendaele

'From the darkness on all sides came the groans and wails of wounded
men; faint, long, sobbing moans of agony and despairing shrieks . . .
and we could do nothing to help them.'

Red-haired, nineteen years old, son of an Irish Custom's officer, living in
Ilford and educated at Stamford Hill School for Roman Catholics, it is not
surprising perhaps that Edwin Vaughan found it difficult sometimes to get
on with his fellow officers. A deep-seated uncertainty covered by an
assertive intolerance must have made him appear cocksure, even arrogant

at times. On 4 January, 1917, however, he entrained for France and started the diary he was to continue daily until August, during which time he matured in its pages from a boy into manhood.

Later in January he was posted to the 18th Warwicks who were in reserve at Abbeville. His first impressions of his fellow officers and the troops were not very favourable. He wrote: 'January 17th. Paraded at 9 a.m. and met my new Company Commander – Lieutenant Hatwell – whom I dislike and despise. He is very small and quite inefficient, though full of bounce and bluff. I knew him very slightly in England. We are the only officers in the Company which consists of badly trained, undisciplined, slovenly men under indifferent N.C.O.'s.'

The following day he revised his opinions slightly: 'I am getting to know the fellows a little better now, but still do not like them very much. I am very disappointed with the Battalion, which in England has always been spoken of as the last word in fighting efficiency.' It was only when he was on the train moving up to the line that he had second thoughts and realized 'that all the empty-headed fellows who had been laughing, joking and drinking ever since I had known them were real soldiers who, after many months in the line, were now returning without the slightest perturbation or nervousness. . . . I began to look around me with a greater interest and more tolerant criticism.'

Even so, he was still unable to appreciate the difference between front-line service and that at base: 'I was astounded this evening on rifle inspection to see Corporal Wood . . . report "all correct" to Sergeant Bell with a cigarette in his hand and his rifle slung. I took Bell sharply to task about it. . . . He raised his eyebrows in blank amazement and replied, "Why, Sir! It's always done up here." I wanted to say, "Well it won't be if I'm on parade," but it would have been subversive of Hatwell's authority so I had to let it pass.'

On 2 February they paraded at 5 p.m. to go up to the front line and 'marched off in fighting order', but his Company was in reserve to carry up rations to the line each night. This supporting role continued with Vaughan's horizons gradually broadening. On 3 February he wrote: 'At 6 p.m. . . . I set out with the Company to carry rations up to the line. . . . As we marched down the exposed lonely road . . . I heard in the far distance a curious musical moan, which with a gradually changing key came nearer and nearer until, immediately overhead, it made a noise like an emptying drain and then died away. . . . I had heard my first shell, and it was quite pretty.'

On 7 February his company was sent up to support the 7th Warwicks. They marched up to the trench-head when he recorded; 'Hatwell told us to wait and then vanished. For three-quarters of an hour we stood in the snow lashed by an icy wind. . . . At last I heard Hatty calling, "Vaughan! Come here damn you!"' He was given orders to take two platoons to Brigade HQ 'for Désirée'.

Eventually Vaughan found the HQ trench and a staff lieutenant named Powell who was reading a novel: 'He took no notice of me until I spoke and then he just glanced up and told me to report to his sergeant. . . . After ten minutes of patient waiting I began to get cross and stamped back . . . to . . . the officer. . . . I told him vehemently 1) That my men had marched a long way and were tired 2) That it was damned cold outside 3) That he had kept them waiting nearly half an hour 4) That there was a war on and 5) That I was entitled to more courtesy than he had shown me. . . . As I was repeating my piece the sergeant came in with a message from the Brigade Major . . . to give us a guide . . . to show us some shelters behind Désirée, where we were to remain as support. . . . When this message was read out I pointed out that my men were still tired, the war was still on, that it was now more damned cold than ever, all because of their inefficiency. Powell gave me a guide and said he would report me to the Brigadier. I said I'd see him in hell and left. My poor frozen troops were led across the open to some shell holes . . . where they crammed in and went to sleep rolled in their greatcoats, while Dunham and I crept into the lousy straw of a tiny shelter and also slept.'

Their shell holes were in full view of the enemy and Vaughan chronicled his views on his batman: 'February 8. This was a bright clear day, but we could not stir out. . . . So I sat . . . and talked to Dunham. He is an oldish and rather dirty-looking fellow, with a long drooping moustache. As a servant he is absolutely useless and was allotted to me by Hatwell because he could not spare a smart man from the Company. Before he joined up he was a lithographer in Dorset; he is quite well spoken and very religious, and although he makes me angry at times, he is very willing and I quite like him.'

The next day they spent in the same way before withdrawing to their billets in the rear and he noted: 'We had no food or water but Dunham got a large chunk of ice out of a shell-hole behind us, so we had some milkless tea. I was a little dubious about using shell-hole water, but it was perfectly white and I should think any germs would be frozen.'

On 14 February, after a few days' rest, they marched up to the front line and Vaughan began to learn the difference between theory and practice. He was detailed for the middle watch of four hours and went with Lieutenant Watkins 'to see the procedure'. After going round the posts they returned to the main trench almost at HQ and he wrote: 'Here I left them re-entering the dug-out to find Hatwell asleep and the servants gone. Helping myself to a large whisky and a chunk of bread and bully, I ... thought of what I had seen. When we had been out of the line I had despised these officers and NCO's and criticized the men, but now I realized that I was the most useless object in the Company. Immediately on entry they had quietly melted away and taken up their duties, already keenly alert and capable, and here was I, still confused, wondering and fearful.'

He sat down and drank several whiskies before dozing off and was finally awakened by Watkins for his tour of duty: 'As my sergeant did not arrive I went out alone to the trench, where the eerie influences of the night descended upon me ... a cold fear chilled my spine and set my teeth chattering. I stood shaking. Then in a panic I sent off down the trench ... to the first post where I stood beside Corporal Bobby Wood until Sergeant Allsop arrived. ... We walked up and down ... until with great relief I saw it was 4 a.m. and I was able to go in and wake Hatwell. After one or two more whiskies I turned in and fell asleep in a moment.'

The next day he was unexpectedly sent to Amiens on a refresher course, and only arrived back at his Company HQ shortly before evening 'Stand-to' on 11 March to find Hatwell had gone and Lieutenant Anstey had taken over the command. His tour of duty started at 10 p.m. and he recorded the session in grim detail for the snow had now gone and the rain had set in:

'Sergeant Hughes was my N.C.O. and I went out into the trench as he arrived. ... The trench sides are falling in and the mud is up to our waists. It is impossible to walk through it and the only way to progress is to bury our arms in the sloppy mud of the trench sides and drag ourselves along. ... As I had not been round the trench on the right I let Hughes take the lead and dragged myself after him for about ten yards. ... The rain was pouring down and we were already soaked through. As we loosened ourselves in the mud, to continue our round, there was a faint "pop" in the distance . . . followed by a rapid whistle and the sharp crack and flash of a bomb bursting about five yards away. Even as we ducked . . . another bomb burst in the same place.'

Sergeant Hughes explained in a whisper that these were *grenaten werfers*, termed 'blue pigeons' or 'pineapples' by the troops, and as the Germans could hear them squelching in the mud they would follow their progress with these. Vaughan continued: 'In no wise cheered by this prediction I told him to push on, and we continued to drag one leg after the other very slowly, ducking every few seconds as a singing, blinding crash flung fifty red-hot fragments about us.'

They crawled in this way for about a hundred yards but in negotiating an old iron pump across the trench Vaughan's tin hat fell off and clanged against it. 'As I stooped to retrieve it, an angry burst of machine-gun fire swept over our heads, whilst a perfect hurricane of bombs fell about us. Several of them fell within two yards of us, but owing to the mud we were unhurt, one dud actually falling between us and a few inches from where our faces were pressed into the side of the trench.'

After another fifty yards 'pursued in terror and with many prostrations' they reached their advance post where 'a voice, low and trembling . . . commanded us to halt. It was Corporal Johnson who told me his post was a few yards further on.' To reach it they had to cross a sunken road commanded by a German machine gun sited only thirty yards away. By rushing over it at full speed both Vaughan and his sergeant got across safely.

He noted, not surprisingly: 'The poor lads in this post were "windy". The long night of rain and darkness, the incessant bursting of pineapples and bursts of gunfire, added to the loneliness, the strain of watching, the enforced silence and the nearness of the Germans, had played havoc with their nerves. I stopped for some time and tried to cheer them up in whispers before I moved forward up the short trench to the post in front.'

Vaughan described this as a circular hole round which the six men lay in a ring. 'Corporal Bennet was in command and he appeared to have thorough wind up. . . . He came after me and asked if he could be relieved as he had lost his nerve. He was shaking with fear and I felt very sorry for him, but knowing . . . that if I showed any clemency the rot would spread, I told him he was to return to his post at once and set an example to his men. . . . Pulling himself together he apologised in a firm voice, saying he could not understand why he had cracked up then, as he had been in much hotter places. . . . I told him not to worry and went on to No 4 post. . . . The trench here . . . was much deeper and the men were fairly well sheltered. . . . After passing the fifth post . . . we were now back in the control trench. . . . Our 300-yard tour of duty had taken 3½ hours and now I just had time to re-visit No 6 post, when my time was up.

'I took Hughes with me into the dugout and poured a stiff tot of rum for each of us; then, sitting by the huge glowing brazier I commenced removing with a stick the two inches of slimy mud that encased me from the waist down and from the shoulders to the wrists. . . . My revolver was choked with mud and I had to clean it before I could turn in. . . . Finally, slightly loosening my equipment, and laying my tin hat and open gas helmet one on either side of my head, soaked and shivering outside, but glowing with rum inside, I fell asleep.'

After Stand-down he learned that Corporal Bennet had been killed soon after he had left him, along with three of his men. The following evening Vaughan buried the four corpses in shellholes behind their post.

The next day, 13 March, just before they were to be relieved, they received a message at 5 p.m. informing them that the heavy artillery would bombard the enemy at 5.20 p.m. and to withdraw the advanced posts. This was impossible in the time allowed and he recorded: 'At 5.20 . . . we waited for the shells to pass over . . . until with devastating crashes they exploded – 30 yards *behind* us! As we stared at each other in horror another salvo came . . . on top of us . . . a terrific crash flung us in all directions and into darkness. It felt quite pleasant to be dead. . . . Just a light singing in my ears, restful blackness around me and a sense of absolute freedom and abandon . . . then I heard a loud crash . . . and Holmes' voice saying, "Is anybody hurt?". . . . I now found that during the few seconds I had believed myself dead, I had closed my notebook, snapped round the elastic and returned the pencil to its socket.'

The shelling had killed Sergeant Bennet, brother of the Corporal killed the previous evening, but after this their relief arrived. Shortly afterwards Anstey handed over command of the Company to Billy Kentish. Under him Vaughan got into hot water with his CO for failing to relieve a platoon in an advanced post, a mistake at least partially his company commander's fault. Then Lieutenant Ewing took over command from Kentish and on another occasion Vaughan and two NCOs were fortunate not to be killed when given an incorrect map reference by him, but all the time he was gaining experience.

On 2 April he was sent with Major Gell to reconnoitre and Vaughan wrote: 'We saw our divisional General 'Dicky' Fanshawe. . . . [He] came galloping back and handed a packet of chocolate to Gell, saying, "This may be useful to you." It is this benevolent habit which has earned him the nickname of "The Chocolate Soldier".'

At this stage they were very short of water for the Germans had contaminated all water supplies. On 4 April he noted: 'It had been raining hard so there were plenty of puddles and we got a good wash. We had not shaved for days and presented a very ragged appearance. Moreover, I had developed a beastly rash over my body.' He was afraid this was scabies, but the doctor subsequently diagnosed it as a rash caused by dirt and vermin.

On 7 April he noted triumphantly: 'The Boche had shelled fairly closely during the night, but no damage was done. I didn't even get the wind up.'

The company was holding a position along a railway cutting and the following day he was standing on the edge of the cutting at dawn 'and I must have let it get too light for . . . a crackle of bullets swept past me. . . . I dropped like a rabbit and rolled down the bank, grabbed a Lewis gun and climbed up again in time see about a dozen Boche hurrying across . . . a thousand yards in front. I gave them a couple of bursts and had the satisfaction of seeing several drop. . . . I returned the gun to its owner and . . . too tired to go round by the road decided to risk it across the top . . . and in safety we crossed the shell-pitted fields. . . . We were perfectly quiet all day and I thoroughly enjoyed wandering around with Kentish and Ewing looking at corpses of Jerries.'

On 14 April they were unexpectedly called on as reserves for an attack, and as such fortunately had few casualties. On then taking over the front line he wrote: 'April 15th, Sunday. At one o'clock, as we waited for the first signs of a Boche counterattack, we heard troops behind us and learnt with delirious joy that it was the 10th Lancs who had been sent up to relieve us. Eagerly we handed over and made off. . . . As I passed through the wire I stopped to free a poor dying bugler-boy. . . . I handed him over to the stretcher-bearers who were now busy amongst the wounded, who lay shrieking and groaning on all sides.'

They returned to Peronne on 19 April where he recorded: 'The mess was ripping. The room I was in had been a shop, now it contained a settee, one arm and four other chairs and two tables. Behind it was a large kitchen with a big open fireplace. . . . During the afternoon a new batch of officers arrived. . . . Jimmy Harding, an oldish fellow, dry and wizened, late champion shot of southern India . . . forthwith nicknamed "the Rajah". Frank Radcliffe, an artistic, quiet, middle-aged man and a Doctor of Music; and then a very young chap named Hammond, an ex-Grenadier Guardsman of splendid stature and physique. . . . Our first dinner was a very jolly meal. Hammond and I went round to the canteen and returned laden with delicacies – curried prawns, tinned fruit and butter, tongue, port and liqueurs, etc. I exerted myself as mess president and when we had had delightful baths, shaves and changes of clothing we sat down to a six-course dinner that prepared us for a long sociable evening round the fire with glasses of port beside us and coronas between our lips. . . . When we went to bed . . . Hammond . . . astounded me by saying . . . he had not long to live for he was eaten up with consumption.'

On 21 April he blithely recorded some looting: 'Radcliffe and I went round scrounging. We went through dozens of houses, climbing over roofs and knocking through walls and ended up with lots of nice cutlery, salt cellars, glasses, etc. . . . We scrounged curtains for our glassless windows and some lamps and tablecloths, so that by evening with our Harrison-Fisher girls framed upon the walls we had a very cosy mess.'

Two days later, after working with the troops from 7 to 11 a.m., he had asked Ewing's permission to go sick so that he could have his teeth checked since they had been troubling him. He was told he would have to go to hospital and so returned to his working party which knocked off at 1 p.m. He then received a summons to report to Major Gell, acting as CO, who reprimanded him in front of the doctor, the padre and the acting adjutant for being absent on parade and general slackness.

Vaughan wrote: 'He added: "Look at your record since you have been with the Battalion. You fall foul of Brigade the first time you report to them; you make a fool of yourself when you take a few men to hand over a position; you lose yourself when you are sent up to find your Company HQ and now you slink away from your work. . . . If you don't pull yourself together with a jerk, you will be sent back to England as an inefficient officer." . . . There was nothing I could say so I saluted and walked slowly back to the billet trying to fight down my angry resentment and depression.'

With the resilience of youth he soon recovered himself and on the following day, 24 April, he wrote: 'Was delighted today to be sent back to . . . the old trenches at Biaches. . . . We went on to . . . where we had had such a rotten time in the line. . . . The German trenches were in perfect condition, deep and beautifully revetted with high fire-steps and pumps. It was a higher site than ours and from their fire position every bit of our line was visible; we could also see that they had pumped all the water from their trenches into ours. . . . I found that at one point we had each had a machine gun staring straight at each other with only twenty yards between. At the point where I had heard the Boche talking I saw that we had been standing against the wall of a cellar in which they were living. . . . The German wire was very thick and in many places he had arranged elaborate bomb-traps to catch raiding parties. I had a look at one old shelter behind Désirée and saw that the one from which Dunham had got the ice for our tea was full of green water in which lay a rotting Frenchman – yet our tea had tasted quite good.'

On 26 April he noted: 'During the afternoon Saunders, the Company sanitary man, digging in the yard behind the Company's billet, struck a bottle of wine. Digging carefully he unearthed a huge dump. . . . Several bottles found their way into our mess, but of course we knew nothing about it officially.'

Almost predictably, next morning he recorded: 'Harding accompanied me today in the road-mending party and, when we went on parade at 7 a.m. we had a terrible shock. There were numerous absentees and nearly everybody was tight. They were reeling about and laughing and presented such an extraordinary sight in two swaying lines that we hurried them off at once. . . . They were immensely happy and greeted everyone we passed – including mules, with most amusing remarks. . . . When we arrived at our working place we spread them out along the road, then discreetly retired to the soberest part. . . . Luckily no one came along to supervise the work so when we marched the fairly sobered company back at midday we said nothing to Ewing.'

On 3 May he recorded: 'In the evening we had a Battalion dinner, all officers dining together at HQ. . . . The dinner was very loud. The food was excellent and the champagne flowed very freely. Nearly everybody got tight, Thomas being the first to succumb. While the CO was making a serious speech, recalling the history of the Battalion . . . Tommy burst into maniacal laughter and collapsed on the floor. He was swept up and Radcliffe took the piano. . . . After a long singsong a violent rag was started. . . . Coleridge and Scales had a serious fight, but neither was hurt and they ended by kissing and crying over each other.'

Their rest period lasted until 13 May when he noted: 'Sunday; We spent the day preparing to move up the line and were given maps of our new position. . . . At dusk we moved off . . . and . . . we . . . had just climbed onto an open plain when the order "Gas Alert" was passed back. We got our gas-masks ready but save for a slight smell of pineapple there was no development.'

He recorded the relief as follows: 'A gradual downward slope . . . brought us to a trench barely 20 yards long. Here an officer greeted me. . . . A small cubby-hole had been scooped into the front of the trench and into this we crawled. There was just room for us to lie full length on the straw, with a candle stuck between us on a piece of stick jabbed into the side. Here I signed for the stores of bombs, Very lights, ammunition and petrol tins which I had checked and I asked . . . if he had any tips . . . about the trench. He told me that everything was very quiet but that no one could move by day. At night Jerry had strong patrols out . . . but his line was a thousand yards away.'

He continued: 'May 14 . . . we being mutually satisfied he led his platoon away and I despatched Dunham to HQ with my "Relief Complete" message. . . . I then met Radcliffe coming to meet me. We . . . decided to break the ice . . . by going out into No Man's Land. I felt awfully frightened and my heart beat very high as for the first time I passed through the wire into the silence and mystery of the unknown ground. The moon was giving a faint light through the clouds which enabled us to see dimly for about 50 yards.

'For about a hundred yards we walked slowly forward, seeing nothing. . . . Then suddenly Radcliffe grasped my arm and pulled me quietly but quickly down into the long grass. Holding my breath I heard a faint but distinct rustle of knees ploughing through clover and then dimly in front I saw a small party of men approaching us. They halted 40 yards away and I lay frozen with fear and excitement . . . [they] moved slowly across to our left . . . whilst we crawled swiftly backwards to the trench.'

A few moments later they saw a Very light go up and the Australians on their left started firing and they saw faint figures running away. 'I took Raddy back to my little cubby-hole where Dunham had laid out my blanket, oilsheet, rations, cigarettes and a bottle of port. We took turns in drinking port from a tin mug, then Raddy went back to his posts and I began to draw a map of the position and made out a report on the patrol. I was so pleased at having broken the ice that I felt quite anxious to get out again with a fighting patrol behind me. I was awake all night visiting the posts ... when day had broken, I curled up in my cubby-hole with Dunham and slept peacefully.'

He described the next day in the trench very fully: 'May 15. At about 12 noon I woke while Dunham still slept. I wormed my way out under the oilsheet which screened the front of our hole and standing erect in the trench I met a fresh sweet breeze and clear warm sunlight that made me glowing and alert in a moment. . . . I dragged the sleeping Dunham by his ankles, upbraiding him for wasting such delightful sunlight – especially when I wanted my lunch. Then I went round the corner to see Corporal Wood. "Bobby" . . . grinned amiably when I appeared. "Bit better than Blighty, don't you think, Sir?" I agreed that there was less worry and certainly more peace and he climbed out of his shelter to stand with me. . . . It was indeed still . . . until without warning there was a mighty crash and a spray of earth and stones fell over us as we flung ourselves against the trench side . . . and as Wood climbed back into his recess, I hurried back to mine – not that these holes afford the slightest protection . . . but as a rabbit seeks his burrow so we each dash to our own hole for safety. Dunham was standing in the trench with a tin of pork and beans . . . the best antidote to fear is food, so we sat on the mouth of our hole and shared a tin of bully and beans and I drank port while Dunham made tea.'

That evening after dark he and Radcliffe went out on patrol with their men. 'We advanced in jumps. Raddy and I creeping forward with a runner scenting the ground for 50 yards at a time and then sending the runner back. . . . After a while . . . we two crept on alone until we reached a junction of two roads. . . . As we approached we heard faint voices and looking over, there . . . were eight or ten large Boche. We . . . crawled off back to the patrol . . . when a figure almost upright hurried past us and was lost in the darkness. So *we* stood up then and ran back to . . . our lads. Quickly we told them what we had seen and in a moment . . . we set off together – out for blood. Alas! When we reached the crossroads nothing remained. . . . We had to be content with firing a few rounds down the road after them, and then we walked back. . . . This little jaunt has left us with our tails well up and I, for one, am very keen on No Man's Land. I fully appreciate the truth of the axiom that was dinned into us during training – "Fighting patrols are the finest stiffeners of morale".

'May 16. The remainder of the night was uneventful except that for a breezy five minutes . . . when one of our own 18-pounder batteries fired 24 shells straight on to our left post. . . . There were no casualties.'

On 19 May: 'Message came up during the evening that we will be relieved tomorrow night. Cheers !! Raddy spent most of the night with me and we ate a lot and drank more – to save carrying things out of the line with us. Dawn was in consequence much rosier and I went to sleep feeling very cheery.'

When they were finally relieved Vaughan and his platoon were detached as 'escort to the guns' of an Australian battery. A month before the previous battery had been attacked by a raiding party of Germans and it was felt necessary to provide them with infantry support. An officer of his regiment was billeted with him and he wrote: 'Berry is a good-hearted chap but very foul-mouthed and loud-voiced. He drinks far too much and when he turned up this evening he was very tight.'

He added: 'I have been particularly struck by the niceness of the Australians' conversation. They never swear and their ordinary talk is very gentle and homely, the kind and intelligent discussions contrasting sharply with the coarse or harsh inanities that resound in the messes of most British units. They seem to have a tremendous respect and admiration for their skipper, too, although they are all so familiar.'

When visiting the Battalion HQ he passed one of the platoons and noted: 'All these lads stood up as we approached and each salute to me was followed by a greeting to Dunham who is immensely popular throughout the Company. . . . Dear old Dunham! He . . . is now my most valuable possession.'

Vaughan learned that they were to return to the front on 29 May and wrote: 'May 28. The usual "day before" – inspections, returns of working strength, etc. There was no excitement as we are familiar with the sector, but I believe my lads are quite pleased to be going back to the wild poppy-covered land of night patrols and daydreams. I know that there is that feeling somewhere in *my* mind.'

He had obviously liked the Australians and the next day wrote: 'I said goodbye to the Australians with real regret, thanking them from the bottom of my heart for their hospitality when I came, a stranger, amongst them. . . . The remainder of the Company came up to us an hour before dusk and we led them on, Ewing walking with me in front. . . . The track that we followed skirted Lagnicourt, which is out of bounds to everybody owing to there being 2,000 dead lying in and around the village.'

While they marched Ewing told him that the platoons were to carry out patrols and Vaughan was inspired to volunteer to do them all. He wrote: 'He jumped at the idea as it will save him a lot of organization and we agreed that provided the CO and, of course, my men were agreeable, I should keep them in the reserve trench with HQ and employ them only on fighting patrols.'

As soon as they had settled in he put the suggestion to his men and noted: 'They simply leapt at it, and I returned well pleased to tell Ewing. He had already received the acquiescence of the CO – so that was that.'

As soon as they were settled in he took his NCOs and three of his men out beyond the wire for a quick reconnaissance from 3 a.m. until near dawn. The next evening he took out his first patrol recording: 'In bunches of six we passed out through the wire. As a preliminary we swept straight across our front in extended order, searching every inch of the ground. . . . Then with infinite caution we advanced into the neutral ground of shadows and mystery, every sense alert for the faintest sign of a German patrol . . . but although we advanced for about 400 yards we saw no Boche and at midnight, in pitch darkness, I led the patrol back.'

He continued: 'I detailed six men to report to me at 4.30 and then dismissed them all to their dugouts where they had (as I had) a wonderful hot meal that had come up in food containers. These containers are a great boon to us, for the food arrives quite hot at the front line. In the past we have had to do any little cooking possible over a Tommy's cooker – if we had one. At 4.30 a.m. I took my six men out again and scoured the whole area again. In such a small party we were able to move much faster and with less caution. We returned just before dawn.'

On 1 June he noted; 'The night patrol was rather dull as we swept the whole of No Man's Land without seeing or hearing anything of the Boche. On the dawn patrol, however, we had a little excitement for we ran suddenly into one of Jerry's patrols. We both opened fire together and, crouching in the long grass, blazed away in the half-light. Jerry retreated and we followed him up until we lost him. We had no casualties and we found no dead or wounded from his party.'

On 2 June he was summoned back to meet his CO, who showed him an air photograph and pointed out a crossroads on it which was a German strongpoint. He was ordered to investigate it thoroughly for a raiding party, taking Radcliffe with him. He recorded events thus: 'June 3. . . . For 500 yards we crawled inch by inch through the darkness, in two parties – each in diamond formation. . . . At last . . . I headed the patrol round to the left. As we moved on there was a sharp crack and a Very light shot up, flooding us in a white light and a burst of rifle fire spat over our heads. I raised myself in time to see a white chalk trench a hundred yards ahead. We . . . continued to crawl to the left until I reached . . . a steep bank almost overhanging the crossroads.'

Ahead of them he could see a belt of wire and the dark holes of the German posts overlooking the road. To go down into the road looked like suicide, but he decided it had to be done. 'Bobby Wood and I together slithered over the bank and down into the road where we lay with faces crushed into the chalk waiting for the clatter of bullets around us . . . but nothing happened. . . . As the truth dawned on me I stood up and in disgust began to hurl large chunks of chalk at the enemy trench.'

The Germans, having heard the firing earlier and fearing an attack, had withdrawn to their rear trenches. Their party was able to destroy a rifle pit and a mine shaft. They then reconnoitred as far as the main German trenches. Finally they returned just before dawn and Vaughan made out a detailed report for HQ.

On 5 June Ewing tore a hole in his leg on a spike and Vaughan wrote: 'I found him waiting for the stretcher to take him down the line . . . evidently in great pain. "Oh Vaughan," he said, "Look after my kit for me and redirect my letters won't ye?" I felt sincerely sorry for him and his last appeal made me realize I would not see him for a long time – perhaps not again – and I know now that I liked him a lot.'

His friend Pepper took over the Company and Vaughan recorded: 'He read me a long lecture, . . . "The CO is always asking for reports about you and has seriously considered sending you back to England. In addition to that the officers of the other companies despise you for your arrogant unsociableness and look upon you as an inefficient young officer." . . . I pointed out . . . I . . . had not had the instruction or support I had expected from my several company commanders. "And," I argued, "surely I can choose my own friends?" "No you can't," he said . . . ". . . you've done nothing, while these others – whatever their characters are – have sweated out here for months and so are entitled not to your friendship, but to your *respect*. . . . There is no room for personal dislikes; if our social relations are bad, we will never work together. . . . And what the devil do you expect your company commander to do for you? Wet nurse you?" . . . However he poured a little oil into the wound by saying, "It may soothe you to know that Colonel Hanson is very pleased with your patrol work. . . . And . . . Berry's platoon is being attached to yours to get used to working in No Man's Land."'

Vaughan recorded that evening: 'Berry's platoon arrived at dusk. . . . I took half a dozen of these fellows out with my patrol. I found . . . that the posts previously occupied were now empty and that others were manned. This confirmed my early conjecture that to puzzle possible raiding parties [Jerry] changed his positions nightly, or bi-weekly. This I entered in a report.'

He was then ordered to report to the CO and wrote: 'I attended the rendezvous with mixed feelings. After a peg of whisky the CO produced an aeroplane photograph and a map and told me to describe . . . my patrol work. . . . A close examination of the aeroplane map confirmed my reports in every detail. . . . As I rose to go . . . he congratulated me. . . . "Keep on like that and you will do well," he added and I . . . walked back on air to HQ trench.'

On 8 June they were relieved and withdrew to the rear area under canvas. Despite the lecture of his friend Pepper he did not try very hard to control his feelings regarding his brother officers. He wrote: 'June 11 . . . All subaltern officers had a lecture this morning on "Discipline". It was given by Captain Taylor of A Company, whom I detest. He wears a quite superfluous eyeglass, is very supercilious and speaks to no one below his own rank. . . . We were delighted when a few shrapnel shells . . . caused him to terminate his harangue.'

They returned to the line on June 13 with Anstey as company commander. 'I took up my old position in HQ trench with Anstey. I am not doing any patrols this tour as A Company are having a turn. . . . I find Anstey very good company in the line, where he treats the whisky bottle with great respect. . . . We . . . had a wonderful time crawling through the long grass playing Indians. . . . Our troops were firmly convinced that their officers did not stand the strain of war very well.'

On 17 June B Company sent out a raiding party with Bridge and Berry to attack the crossroads. Vaughan noted: 'At 10.30 p.m. the attacking party arrived. . . . Bridge was quite calm and stolid, Berry loud and excited. . . . At 11 o'clock . . . the crackle of rifle fire and quick crashes of bombs told us that the raid had commenced. . . . Hearing voices in front I went out through the wire. It was an enormous Hun prisoner escorted by two of our fellows. He was very unhappy. . . . Then the raiding party began to trickle through, all very pleased with themselves.'

The next day he recorded: 'Anstey told me great interest had been aroused by the fact that the large prisoner from the raid had had a dum-dum bullet in the chamber of his rifle. This was alleged to be the first red-handed catch of the war.'

On 19 June he wrote: 'At 4 a.m. leaning over the parapet I had a fine view of Jerry's line and got my first real sight of Prouville by daylight. A charming little village. . . . With my glasses I could discern figures moving in the streets. . . . I borrowed a rifle and had a few pots at long range. . . . After this little attack on enemy morale I . . . breakfasted off tinned herrings and sherry. Then I went to sleep.'

They were relieved again on 23 June and had a spell in the grounds of a large ruined château, where Ewing rejoined them and took over the Company again. After another uneventful spell in the line they had a lengthy march to Berles-au-Bois in the rear area, where they were installed in barns and stables attached to a small estaminet. Vaughan recorded: 'We spent two wonderful weeks in Berles training or (more accurately) fattening up for our entry into the projected advance at Ypres. The weather was perfect and our days and nights were spent in unalloyed content.'

During this period he noted; 'Hammond came in to say goodbye. Consumption had got him down and he was returning to England. . . . Ewing and I learnt to understand one another and became good friends. Our temperaments were very much alike and all the time we had been together a slight hostility had been increased by our nervousness and self-consciousness. This, however, was now cast aside and we lived in perfect harmony.'

Vaughan was particularly pleased to win the confidence of Taylor, 'the black sheep' of his platoon, who had been in prison several times. He noted proudly: 'From that day on we were fast friends and he and his pal Dawson were two of my smartest men.' They were all very keyed up, but he recorded; 'On the whole there was very little drunkenness. Radcliffe got out of hand one night and insisted on visiting every mess in turn, getting tighter and tighter and, I'm afraid, being musically vulgar.'

On 29 July they arrived at a camp near Poperinghe. Vaughan and Radcliffe went into Poperinghe itself and noted: 'It is well within the range of Jerry's guns and the station and square receive frequent reminders of the fact. . . . Along the Ypres road, opposite the station we found the officer's club – a most inviting and comfortable place with a verandah in front where we lounged in deck chairs and drank whisky. . . . Our next visit was to a cafe in the square – La Poupée. . . . We found a table in the glass-roofed garden. . . . We had a splendid dinner and several bottles of bubbly . . . cigars and liqueurs. . . . At 10.30 we rose to leave.'

On 31 July he was unexpectedly given leave and went home to England from 1 to 7 August, returning finally to his Battalion on 10 August, a day late owing to 'the presence of submarines in the channel'. On 13 August he noted: 'We heard this morning that we are moving up again tomorrow and that on the 16th we will be in support to a battalion of Irish Rifles at St. Julien. . . . Before noon we had learnt every detail of the ground from the map and incidentally had been issued with private's clothing. After lunch Radcliffe, Harding and I went down to Pop for a farewell dinner. We have heard so much now, that we know what we are in for. . . . At La Poupée we had a most wonderful dinner with many drinks so that when we started back we were all a little unsteady.'

On 15 August he wrote: 'The whole day we were busy, examining gas-masks, rifles, Lewis guns, field dressings, iron rations, identity disks, etc. and trying to joke with the troops despite the gnawing apprehension that was numbing our minds. Early in the evening I changed into Tommy's uniform and tried to prepare for every contingency – spare laces and string in one pocket, spare pencils in another, scissors in my field dressing pochette, rations and cigarettes in my haversack with my maps, small message maps stuffed into my respirator satchel and a pocketful of revolver ammunition. . . . We handed our money and decent cigarette cases to CQMS Braham so that if anything happened to us Jerry would not have them. Then we mingled with the troops and talked lightly of tomorrow's excitement.'

On 16 August at 2 a.m. they set off with a guide and eventually crossed a canal where they halted and he noted: 'We were at Bridge 2A of the Yser canal, a few hundred yards north of Ypres. The air was poisoned by a terrible stench . . . in the dim light the water appeared to be a dark-green swamp wherein lay corpses of men and bodies of horses, shafts of waggons and gun wheels protruded from the putrefying mass and after a shuddering glance I hurried along the towpath to clearer air.

'Our cookers now rolled up and the cooks carried a hot meal over. . . . For my part I had lost my fear now and in spite of the imminent attack and the fearful mass below me, I ate a hearty breakfast of sausages and bacon. Then as the sky grew light I walked along the path to where

Sergeant-Major Chalk was standing on the bank silhouetted against the sky.'

The Sergeant-Major asked him the time and Vaughan wrote: '"Four forty-five," I said, and with my words the whole earth burst into flame with one tremendous roar as hundreds of guns hurled the first round of the barrage. An instant's pause then far in the distance we saw the faint line of fire where the shells were falling . . . then Chalk tugged my sleeve to indicate that our Company was lining up on the towpath. Scrambling down I slipped on my equipment as I ran forward to fall in beside Ewing. Then in a file we moved forward . . . not a shell fell near us until we reached a sleeper track, which Ewing told me was Buff's Road. Here we formed fours and marched on and on.'

They came to some of the concrete pillboxes about which they had heard, where Colonel Hanson gave Ewing orders. Vaughan went on: 'He led us off the road . . . and gave the signal for artillery formation. . . . We continued to move steadily across that muddy waste until I realized that we were walking into a curtain of fire. We were right on top of the German barrage when glancing round I saw Ewing give the signal to halt. I repeated the signal to my men and we all dived into shell-holes. . . . I lay blinking into the shrieking, crashing hail of death just 30 yards in front. We were too close to fear anything except a direct hit and, fascinated, I stared at that terrible curtain through which we soon must pass.'

A runner tumbled into his shell-hole, '– for now machine gun bullets were sweeping over us – and told me Ewing wanted me to send a patrol to find Border House, which, when located, I was to occupy. I sent Corporal Wood . . . and, having watched him disappear into the barrage, I sat down to await his return. It only seemed a few minutes before he returned, saying he had found it, but one man had been killed.'

The time had come to advance into the barrage and Vaughan wrote: 'Dully I hoisted myself out of the mud and gave the signal to advance, which was answered by every man rising and stepping unhesitatingly into the barrage. The effect was so striking that I felt no more that awful dread of the shellfire, but followed them calmly into the crashing, spitting hell. . . . The men were wonderful! . . . Whilst many were blown over . . . no one was touched until we were through the thickest part of the barrage and making for the little ridge in front. Then I saw fellows drop lifeless, while others began to stagger and limp; the fragments were getting us and in front was a belt of wire.

'At this moment I felt my feet sink and . . . I was dragged down to the waist in sticky clay. The others passed on not noticing my plight until by yelling and firing my revolver in the air I attracted the attention of Sergeant Gunn, who returned and dragged me out. I caught up with the troops and I was following Corporal Breeze when a shell burst at his feet. As I was blown backwards I saw him thrown into the air to land at my feet a crumpled heap of torn flesh. Sick with horror, I scrambled over him and stumbled down into the cutting which was Steenbeck Stream. Crouched in here we found the Irish Rifles and we lined up with them.'

Vaughan saw a padre who grinned cheerfully at him and a Major smoking a pipe and reported to him. 'Then, from the heap of flesh that had been Breeze, I saw the stump of an arm raised an inch or two. Others saw it too and before I needed to tell them the stretcher bearers were on their way to him. Very gently they brought him to where I was sitting. He was terribly mutilated, both his feet had gone and one arm, his legs and trunk were torn to ribbons and his face was dreadful. But he was conscious and as I bent over him I saw in his remaining eye a gleam of mingled recognition and terror. His feeble hand clutched my equipment and then the light faded from his eye. The shells continued to pour but we gave poor Breezy a burial in a shellhole and the padre read a hurried prayer.'

By this time they had lost touch with the rest of the company so Vaughan sent Dunham back to report their position and ask for instructions. Dunham returned to say that 14 platoon were on their left and to stand firm. 'So I told my fellows to make themselves at home in the mud and crawled myself from hole to hole until I came to Jimmy Harding with the remains of his platoon. . . . The shelling now fell away until it was negligible and before long Jimmy was cracking jokes. . . . At about 3 p.m. we saw two figures walking back behind us and, recognizing Radcliffe, we . . . ran across. His right wrist had been shattered by a sniper's bullet and he was very upset for it was a rotten sort of blighty for a Doctor of Music to get. With him was Sergeant Bell who had got a bullet in the arm from the same sniper. It was with real regret we gripped their left hands and said goodbye – we knew for ever. We felt that this was the beginning of the break-up and we rejoined our troops in deep depression.'

Then Ewing arrived and handed over command of the company to Vaughan as he was replacing the Adjutant, Hoskins, who had been hit. He said that Anstey had been badly hit. Vaughan's orders were to move the

Company to the left behind the Gloucesters at dusk and after dark to deal with any machine guns in front.

They found that the noise they made advancing in the mud and water was so great that they had no chance of attacking the guns successfully. On his return from patrol Vaughan found his C O waiting for him. 'I sat down in the mud beside him feeling dead beat and horribly ill. What he was saying I had no idea for I must have fainted, or gone to sleep. . . . He shook me violently and said, "Now Vaughan pull yourself together". Where-upon I was alert in a moment. . . . I was to form up my platoons in depth to the right of where we were then sitting. The Gloucesters were going out before dawn and the following night I was to spread out to the left and form a line joining the Ox and Bucks. Then he left me and I sat for a while staring into the darkness, realizing that we were in a hell of a place.'

He called the Company together and, with Sergeant-Major Chalk, looked for an H Q. They saw a derelict tank which looked as if it might be suitable: 'As we approached it, however, we were met by a filthy over-powering stench and found that a shell had burst underneath it and it had burnt out. Three charred bodies of the crew were inside it or half out of the open door. So I sought the healthier atmosphere of a large crater 30 yards away and gathered my staff in neighbouring shell-holes. . . .

'August 17. It was dawn when I dropped into my shell-hole where Dunham had shaped a great armchair for me in mud. I stared vacantly at the . . . mound behind me . . . until I became aware that I was staring into the face of a dead Tommy, upside down. . . . He had a diamond-shaped hole in his forehead through which a little pouch of brains was hanging and his eyes were hanging down; he was very horrible, but I soon got used to him.'

The chaos of war did not only affect one side. 'At about 3 p.m. I heard the German guns open. . . . As salvo after salvo poured over I got my glasses onto the spot and saw that they were pounding their own line. Soon a line of figures appeared running out of the shelled zone; im-mediately our machine guns opened and mowed them down. I felt terribly sorry for them, for they looked very new and untried and I was so tired and weary myself.'

When night fell the rations were brought up and the C O appeared. 'The C O seemed very strange; he was quiet and sometimes incoher-ent. . . . He told me he wanted me to pace out the exact distance from my front post to the remains of the second hedge in front of St. Julien and let him know before morning. . . . As he crawled out he said, "We've just had a shell on HQ." I asked who was hurt and he replied, 'I think everyone has got it except Ewing." As he stumbled away I saw him bowled over three times by shells before he was lost in the darkness. . . . I was very windy about pacing out the exact distance, but following his example I started out alone. Pacing along the shattered road in the darkness I felt terribly lonely and horrified lest the heavy shelling should catch me and leave me there to rot – just another body. But I found the hedge and returned safely to reward myself with a long swig of whisky.'

He made contact with the Ox and Bucks on his left and got their positions marked on his map. After a hazardous journey he returned to his shell-hole and wrote: 'Dunham was quite alarmed at my absence for like a fool I had omitted to tell anyone where I was going. I remained . . . for half an hour eating the rain-soaked bread and sandbaggy cheese and drinking some cold tea out of a petrol can. Then I lit a cigarette under my oilsheet and had a peg of whisky, after which I set off to find Jimmy Harding.'

In his diary he recorded: 'August 18. Poor old Rajah! He was absolutely whacked. All his spirit had gone and he sat at the bottom of his shell-hole staring dully up at me and hardly speaking . . . so I left him and went round the line talking to the troops. But everywhere was the same dullness and depression and my heart sank more and more.'

A message arrived informing him that they were to be relieved that night and, after a day of intermittent shelling, he wrote: 'When it was dark enough I passed forward from shell-hole to shell-hole arranging for the relief . . . everybody wore that mask of tiredness and complete indifference which I knew was drawn across my soul. But I tried to be easy and natural and at last I found a spark of humanity still glowing in the soul of Bobby Wood. . . . We talked and even laughed a little as we walked over to warn the Ox and Bucks that we were being relieved. . . .

'August 19. Sunday. At Vanhuele Farm we met Samuel who was waiting in the rain for the companies to report "Relief Complete". . . . A voice called out. "Is that you, Vaughan?" and there was dear old Ewing waiting to lead me back. I was jolly glad to see him but . . . unable to talk . . . I was directed to my tent . . . and I sat down and cut my puttees off with a knife. . . . I got into pyjamas and ate my stew lying in bed. It was wonderful to have a hot meal . . . after my four days of nibbling at filth. . . . Sleep mercifully claimed me.'

They were in one of the many camps at Reigersburg about 300 yards out of Ypres. 'August 20. My next few days were very busy. I had casualty returns to render, deficiences to replace, reorganization to carry out and – worst of all – letters to write to the relatives of the fellows who had been killed. In my leisure time I would go for a stroll with Jimmy or Pepper, or lie smoking to watch Jerry trying to hit the road junction.'

On 23 August there was a gas alarm: 'The air faintly charged with a sweet scent of peppery butterscotch. I put on my gas-mask and went round the tents to find the men wearing theirs and playing at being lions and bears.' On 24 August they received details of the next attack planned, in which he was to command C Company in support. He was detailed to take C Company up the next day and to 'work each night on improving the shell-holes' to receive the Battalion, camouflaging the work before dawn so that the Germans would not know of it.

On 25 August: 'Having dressed in my Tommy's uniform and made personal preparations for the attack I led C Company out at dusk to bridge 2A which we crossed at 8 p.m. . . . I had only one officer in the Company – a quiet fellow named Wood. . . . Through an avenue of shell-bursts we reached . . . the concrete blockhouse which was to be our shelter. It was a very long pillbox in which a corridor opened into about eight baby elephant cubicles. The 5th Warwicks were holding the line and Major Bloomer and his staff had one of these cubicles . . . the next I took for Wood and myself. Into the remainder I crammed three platoons. . . . Then I went back and reported myself to Major Bloomer. He was a ripping fellow, so chummy and utterly unruffled that it was difficult to believe that he had been sitting under Ypres conditions for four days.'

On 26 August he noted: 'Sunday. The limber did not arrive at all so no preparations were made for the incoming troops. I did not get any sleep. It rained heavily all night and when I went out at dawn I found the shell-holes filled to the brim with water. . . . At 10.30 our battalion rolled up and was led to their forming-up position. . . .

'August 27. Just after midnight I made my way over to the Boilerhouse where Pepper now had his HQ. He was in fairly cheerful mood but ridiculed the idea of attempting the attack. The rain had stopped for the time being, but the ground was utterly impassable, being covered with water for thirty yards at a stretch in some places and everywhere shell-holes full of water. . . . While we were talking a message arrived from Brigade. "There is a nice drying wind. The attack will take place. . . ." Pepper read this out to me in a tone which implied "This is the end of us".'

The previous evening he had noted: 'Wood, who appeared to me all along to be very windy, was now absolutely helpless. . . . I gave him whacking doses of rum until he went to sleep.' Now he wrote: 'Wood was still lying on his bed in a fuddled state and as I turned in I thought to myself bitterly, "What chance have we got . . . tomorrow? My only officer out of action already and me commanding a company in which I don't know a single man . . . Thank God Merrick is a Sergeant-Major I can hang my shirt on.'

The following morning at 1.45 the time for the advance came and he noted: 'Feeling icy cold from head to foot I took my troops out and through the ominous silence of the bright midday we advanced in line to the Steenbeck Stream. . . . Instantaneously the enemy barrage crashed upon us and even as I rose, signalling my men to advance, I realized that the Germans must have known of our attack and waited at their guns. . . . It only took us five minutes to reach the Boilerhouse, but during that time I saw with a sinking heart that the lines had wavered, broken and almost disappeared. . . .

'At the Boilerhouse I sent Wood on to the gunpits with three platoons, while I grouped my HQ staff under shelter of the concrete wall before reporting to the CO. . . . The hours crept on . . . sick with uncertainty and apprehension the CO, Mortimore, Coleridge and I were huddled in the tiny cubicle of HQ [when] a runner arrived with a report from Taylor that the attack was completely held up: "casualties very heavy".'

It was by this time 6.30 p.m. 'With a grey face' the CO instructed Vaughan to go forward and see what he could do to help at the gunpits. . . . 'He added forlornly, "Good luck".' Vaughan continued: 'I called up my HQ staff and told them we were making for the gunpits, warning them to creep and dodge the whole way. Then I ran across the road and dived into the welter of mud and water followed by Dunham and – at intervals – by the eight signallers and runners. . . . Immediately there came the crackle of bullets and mud was spattered over me as I ran, crawled and dived into shellholes, over bodies, sometimes up to the armpits in water, sometimes crawling on my face along a ridge of slimy mud around some crater.'

Vaughan saw two men killed in the gunpits as he approached and continued: 'I had almost reached the gunpits when I saw Wood looking at me and actually laughing at my grotesque capers. Exhausted by my efforts, I paused a moment in a shell-hole; in a few seconds I felt myself sinking and, struggle as I might, I was sucked down until I was firmly gripped round the waist and still being dragged in. The leg of a corpse was sticking out of the side and frantically I grabbed it; it wrenched off and, casting it down, I pulled in a couple of rifles and yelled to the troops in the gunpit to throw me more. Laying them flat I wriggled over them and dropped half-dead into the wrecked gun position.'

He reported to Taylor, noting: 'I was filled with admiration at the calm way in which he stood, eyeglass firmly fixed in his ashen face. He told me that the attack had not even reached the enemy front line and that it was impossible to advance across the mud. Then he ordered me to take my Company up the hard road to the Triangle and to attack Springfield. He gave his instructions in such a matter of fact tone that I did not feel alarmed. . . . Of all my HQ staff only Dunham was left – the others had been picked off. . . . So many of our men had been killed . . . that Wood and I could only collect a very few.'

Their advance was chaotic. 'Finally Wood and I led 15 men over to the tanks. The fire was still heavy, but now in the dusk and heavy rain the shots were going wide. As we reached the tanks, however, the Boche hailed shrapnel upon us and we commenced rapidly to have casualties . . . only by cursing and driving could my wonderful Sergeant-Major Merrick and myself urge them out of the shelter of the tanks.'

Death and destruction were all around. 'Up the road we staggered, shells bursting around us. A man stopped dead in front of me and, exasperated, I cursed him and butted him with my knee. . . . Very gently he said, "I'm blind, Sir," and turned round to show me his eyes and nose torn away by a piece of shell. "Oh God, I'm sorry, sonny," I said. "Keep going on the hard part," and left him staggering back in his darkness.'

His description of the advance was clearly imprinted on his mind: 'In shell-holes where they had crawled for safety were wounded men . . . and they cheered us faintly as we passed. . . . A tank had churned its way slowly round behind Springfield . . . a moment later I looked and nothing remained of it but a crumpled heap of iron . . . ploughing across the final stretch of mud I saw grenades bursting around the pillbox and a party of British rushed in from the other side. As we all closed in, the Boche garrison ran out with their hands up; in the confused party I recognized Reynolds of the 7th Battalion. . . . We sent the 16 prisoners back . . . but they had only gone a hundred yards when a German machine-gun mowed them down.'

He held a conference with Reynolds and they formed a line with the pill-box as Vaughan's HQ. 'I found the interior in a horrible condition; water, in which floated indescribable filth, reached to our knees; two dead Boche lay face downwards and another lay across a wire bed . . . the stench was nauseating. . . . On one of the machine-gun niches lay an unconscious German officer, wearing two black and white medal ribbons; his left leg was torn away . . . only a few shreds of bone and muscle held it on. A tourniquet had been applied but had slipped. . . . I commenced at once to readjust it . . . reassuring him, I made him comfortable, arranging a pillow out of a Boche pack.'

They had a further alarm when German troops were seen approaching, but they were merely trying to surrender. 'The poor devils were terrified; suspicious of a ruse, I stared into the darkness, while I motioned them back against the wall with my revolver. They thought I was going to shoot them and one little fellow fell on his knees babbling about his wife and *"Zwei kinder"*. . . . The prisoners clustered round me, bedraggled and heartbroken, telling me of the terrible time they had been having. *"Nichts essen"*, *"Nichts trinken"*, always shells, shells, shells. They said that all of their company would willingly come over. . . . I put them into shell-holes with my men who made a great fuss of them, sharing their scanty rations with them.'

The German officer was of sterner stuff. 'I found the Boche officer quite talkative. He told me how he had kept his garrison fighting on and would never have allowed them to surrender. He had seen us advancing and was getting his guns on to us when a shell from the tank had come through the doorway, killed two men and blown his leg off. . . . His voice trailed away and he relapsed into a stupor. . . . So I went out again into the open and walked along our line.'

Perhaps the worst part of the whole nightmare now arose. 'From the darkness on all sides came the groans and wails of wounded men; faint, long, sobbing moans of agony and despairing shrieks. It was too horribly obvious that dozens of men with serious wounds must have crawled for safety into new shell-holes and now the water was rising about them, and, powerless to move, they were slowly drowning. And we could do nothing to help them. Dunham was crying quietly beside me and all the men were affected by the piteous cries.'

At 11.15 they heard the squelching of boots approaching and Vaughan thought they were being attacked from the rear. 'I dashed back yelling a challenge. I was answered by Coleridge who had brought up a company of the 4th Berks. "To reinforce us?" I asked. "No, to relieve you" – and my heart leapt. "We are going back to Reigersburg." . . . I told Wood to carry out the relief of the line and march the troops back. . . . Then I handed over to the company commander. . . . When we had walked round the line, I picked up Coleridge and . . . started back.'

On the way back he noted, 'The cries of the wounded had much diminished now and . . . the reason was only too apparent, for the water was right over the tops of the shell-holes. From survivors there still came faint cries and loud curses . . . often we stopped to drag them up on to the ridges of earth. We lied to them that the stretcher-bearers were coming and most resigned themselves to a further agony of waiting.'

When he returned to Battalion HQ in the Boilerhouse he recorded: 'At its entrance was a long mound of bodies. Crowds of Berks had run there for shelter and had been wiped out by shrapnel. I had to climb over them to enter HQ and as I did so a hand stretched out and clung to my equipment. Horrified I dragged a living man from amongst the corpses. . . . I crawled into the HQ cubicle where Colonel Hanson and Mortimore were sitting; the CO looked years older. My face was a mask of mud and I had to tell them who I was and that we had got Springfield.'

He was told to report the situation to the Brigade HQ and he continued: 'I went out and walked with Coleridge down the shell-swept road to St. Julien . . . a regular hail of shells. . . . But we were past caring and walked through them unscathed. . . . Our runner was killed and we dragged him into a hole.'

He reported to Brigade HQ and finally staggered back to his tent in Reigersburg 'soaked in mud and blood from head to foot. It was brightly lit with candles and Martin had laid out my valise and pyjamas. As I dragged off my clothes he entered and filled my canvas bath with hot water. Doggedly driving all thoughts out of my head I bathed, crawled into bed, ate a large plateful of stew. Then I laid my utterly vacuous head upon the pillow and slept.'

The aftermath in the morning was sickening. 'At about 9 a.m. I dragged myself wearily out to take a muster parade on which my worst fears were realized. Standing near the cookers were four small groups of bedraggled, unshaven men from whom the quartermaster sergeants were gathering information concerning any of their pals they had seen killed or wounded. It was a terrible list. Poor old Pepper had gone – hit in the back by a chunk of shell; twice buried as he lay dying in a hole. . . . Ewing, hit by machine-gun bullets, had lain beside him for a while. . . . Chalk had been seen to fall riddled with bullets; then he too had been hit by a shell. . . . My black sheep – Dawson and Taylor – had died together and of our happy little band of 90 men only 15 remained. . . . Feeling sick and lonely, I returned to my tent to write out my casualty report and instead I sat on the floor and drank whisky after whisky as I gazed into a black and empty future.'

There Vaughan's diary ends abruptly. As far as is known he never wrote another thing. He did, however, attain the rank of captain and gained the M C later in the war. He left the army and married, eventually having four children, but did not find it easy to adjust readily to civilian life. He joined the R A F and qualified as a pilot attaining the rank of Flight Lieutenant in 1928, although forced to retire through ill-health. In 1931, aged only 33, he died in hospital after a faulty injection and his diaries remained undiscovered until 1981.

Bibliography

Campbell, Colonel Walter: *My Indian Journal*: Edmonstone & Douglas: 1864:

Coppard, George: *With a Machine Gun to Cambrai*: HMSO: 1969:

Godward, Charles: *Diaries & Letters*: Unpublished:

Pester, John: *An Officer's Diary: War & Sport in India*: 1802–1806: Heath Cranston & Ouseley: 1913:

Schaumann, August: *On the Road with Wellington: The Diary of a War Commissary in the Peninsular Campaigns*: Ed & Translated by Anthony M. Ludovici: 1924:

Simmons, Major George: *A British Rifle Man: Journals & Correspondence during the Peninsular War and Campaign of Wellington*: Ed: Lt Colonel Willoughby Verner. Greenhill Books: 1899:

Vaughan, Edwin Campion: *Some Desperate Glory: The diary of a young officer 1917*: Leo Cooper: 1981: